Not Bad for an
AMISH Boy

Memoirs of Eli A. Helmuth

Eli A. Helmuth

Not Bad for an Amish Boy

Carlisle Printing
WALNUT CREEK

2673 TR 421
Sugarcreek, OH 44681

Dedication

I want to dedicate this book to my dear wife, Martha, who stood by me these many years, and to my seven children: Jacob Helmuth, Bill Helmuth, Carolyn Helmuth, Betty Kaetterhenry, Edna Gingerich, Martha Major, Bonnie Yoder, and to their partners. Also to our foster daughter, Clara Louise Yoder.

Without their help and encouragement, this book would never have been written.

Contents

1

An Amish Boy

Childhood and Growing-up Years

I was born on June 6, 1918 to Alvin and Lizzie Helmuth, an Amish couple in Plain City, Ohio. We lived at 9880 Smith-Calhoun Rd. on the farm later owned by Mrs. John Gingerich, 2 miles southeast of Plain City.

My father was the son of Samuel Helmuth. My mother was the daughter of Benjamin Frey, one of the first settlers in the Plain City area. I had four sisters and four brothers. In order we were: Emma, Martha, Dan and Fannie (twins), Eli, Ben, Katie, Al and Jonas.

My parents were fairly strict Old Order Amish and were farmers. We were in the East Amish district where Jacob Farmwald was bishop. We had no electricity, no telephone, no tractors, and no gas engines. Everything was done by hand and horsepower. Hand pumps and a windmill supplied our water. We had oil lanterns, and later, gas lanterns. We had no washing machine; all the washing was done by hand.

We had no toilet or bath in the house. We had to walk about 100 feet to the outhouse, furnished with Sears Roebuck catalogues because we did not have toilet paper. The outhouse was also a resting place where we could look through the catalogues. Walking to the outhouse at night with no lights was not very desirable. We boys sometimes just opened the upstairs windows until Mom spotted yellow streaks on the house siding. That put a stop to that!

One of our late night jobs was to walk across the road to shut the windmill off. The milk trough was filled by pumping water by hand. We took turns, each pumping a hundred strokes. On the average we had twenty cows, twenty horses and around twenty sows, many sheep and around 400 hens.

I had to wear a dress until I was about three years old. My mother must have had a hard time toilet-training me. That was customary in those days. It was a little embarrassing when Mom took me to town with her. The storekeeper would say, "What is your little girl's name? She is cute."

Saturday evening, the water was heated in two iron kettles in the washhouse. A large tub was close by, and hot water from the kettles was put in the tub. We all had to take turns to get our weekly bath. Our time allotment was about 10 minutes each. Then it was time for Saturday night supper, maybe apple dumplings, or corn bread and beans.

For Sunday morning breakfast we always had coffee soup. After the milking was done and all the chores done, it was time to get ready for church. Church was held every two weeks, and we had no Sunday School. We still had some mud roads, so we had two horses hitched to a surrey buggy. Eight-thirty was the time to leave, as church started at 9:00 a.m. The singing would start, and the preachers would proceed upstairs to counsel. After 3 or 4 songs, the preachers would come down.

The women sat in one room and the men in another room. The boys would sit separately in the back room and sometimes were a little noisy. I sat with Mom until about age three, then sat with Dad. Cookies were passed at about 10:30. It was a sad day when Dad told me I was too old to take a cookie! One preacher would have the 'awfang' (beginning), then the Deacon would read scripture and lead in prayer, and then the main sermon was preached. The services were all in German, and the teaching at that time was pretty much about good works. Yes, they taught that Christ was born and died on the cross, but no assurance of salvation. At about 12:00 noon he sat down, and the church sang one song. Then the Bishop would get up again and make the announcements. Sometimes it was for members to stay in for counseling or other things. He would announce where church was to be held in 14 days. Then we were dismissed.

The men put two benches together for a table and two benches to sit on. The women set up the meal. The meal consisted of bread and peanut butter, apple butter, pickles, 'roht-reeva' (pickled beets), and coffee. The women were escorted to one room to prepare tables and the men to another room. The children up to about age 7 or 8 would eat with their parents. After that age, boys would go to one table and girls to another table. At those tables it was pretty lively.

It was quite a chore sometimes for a mother with 2 or 3 children at her side to keep them fed with bread and peanut butter, etc. After dinner, lots of visiting was done. Then we would hitch up the horses and be off for home. It had been a well-spent day.

When I was two years old, some of my sisters were taking water by horse and buggy out to the field for the thresher men for drinking. They took me along. On the way back they happened to hit a post, and I fell off and had a deep gash in my forehead. I still carry the mark. Bleeding could not be stopped for a few days. That is when it was discovered that I was a hemophiliac, lacking a certain clotting factor. Mom told me they almost lost me. But they did finally get the bleeding stopped. I have had many narrow escapes in my life, and I will write about those as I go along.

Now at three years of age I had graduated from a dress to pants, suspenders and a shirt made from dyed 'Wayne' feed sacks. I bet I looked like a little dutchman. All our 'everyday' shirts and the girls' dresses were made from feed sacks. My mother told me at three and four I loved to gather the eggs, sometimes throwing one at something. One highlight was when Dad told me if I went and changed clothes, he would take me with him to town. That was super because Dad loved his chocolate drops, so that meant candy for me also. I have always been a lover of candy.

Our daily schedule was as follows: Get up at 5 a.m., take the lanterns to the chicken houses, go to the barn, and call the horses and cows. Usually when we whistled and called for them, they would come up to the barn from the pasture. One boy would feed the horses and cows. The others would curry and harness horses, anywhere from 10 to 18 horses, depending on what the work schedule was for the day.

Mom and the girls would get breakfast ready. We boys would then go to the house for breakfast. Usually our breakfast consisted of fried corn mush and liverwurst, biscuits and gravy, or eggs and sausage.

After breakfast we boys got the horses and went to the field, and Mom and the girls did the milking. Dad fed the hogs, the sheep and the chickens.

Dad was a big farmer with horses. We farmed the home farm, the Torbert land across from Sam Torbert's, the Tagert land which was across the creek from Amity, the Cary land behind Burl Mayer's, the land where Pleasant Valley Senior Center now is, and the land along the railroad by the boat factory. He also farmed the land owned then by Charles Grubb where Madison Square now is.

My father was also known for his fine horses. We always had a few colts running around. We had a lot of horsemen stopping in, like Rodney Bidwell and Henry Conklin.

At about age 6, my job in the mornings was to carry in a bucket of cobs to start a fire in the wood cook stove. I split wood for the kitchen stove and filled the woodbox in the living room for the wood heater. I also had to keep the reservoir on the kitchen range filled with water. That was the water supply for us to wash up with when we came in from the chores. We had a large bell on a post that the women rang when dinner or supper was ready.

I started to go to school at age 6, but could not speak English. My teacher's name was Mrs. Wozencraft. I did not like school, because I was made fun of. My classmates insisted my dad had put a crock over my head and then cut around the crock. There was one boy who would side with me. He later became my marble-playing buddy. He was Warren Moore. He was a black boy, and I was Amish. We were good friends and still are to this day.

In 1926, at 8 years of age, I was now old enough to drive a team of horses. My first driving experience was driving a two-horse team hitched to a cultivator. We had a single-row corn cultivator where I sat on the seat and drove. My brother Dan walked behind and guided the shovels with handlebars. A few years later we got modern and went to a riding cultivator.

I remember one time we were cultivating and heard a loud noise overhead. We looked up and saw this huge thing. It looked like a large bird. We both ran over to the fence row and hid under the weeds until it had passed. That night at the supper table the others told us it had been an airplane.

After the day's work we did the chores and the milking. Then we would go to the house at 7:00 for a big supper. At 8:00 we would "hit the sack", and I mean sack, on a mattress filled with cut straw from the straw shed. I can't remember anyone in the family having a backache.

A knock on the stovepipe or the upstairs door was our signal to get up in the morning. "Boova, "sis zeit fa ufshtay." (It's time to get up, boys)

"Oh, Dad, it's too early," but we knew Dad meant what he said. Downstairs we'd go. "Dad, what's the menu for today?" One 4-horse team for the disc, one 4-horse team for the harrow, and a 3-horse team for the grain drill. That would be eleven horses to harness and get ready.

At 6:30, after doing the chores and breakfast, off we would go to the Tagert land down across the creek from Amity and the covered bridge. Ben had one team with the disc, Dan did the drilling, and I had one team with the harrow. The drilling was heavy work because the fertilizer came in 125-pound bags. We liked that area because we could walk across the bridge to the Bishop's Grocery store to get three large Mr. Goodbars for a dime. One bar each for Dan, Ben and me. At noon while the horses ate and rested, we took a nudist dip in the creek.

Dad came down to inspect and said, "Boova, sell is goot." (Well-done, boys) Dad always complimented us.

That evening we gathered in again. After supper and thanking the Lord for His blessings, we were again ready to "hit the sack". "Al, you go shut the windmill off, the other boys worked hard," Dad said.

The next morning we woke up at 5:00, and it was raining. "Good, we can have a little more time in bed!" We got up at 5:30, did the chores and had breakfast. Today we would work around the barn and do odd jobs. The rain had stopped, so we could do odd jobs outside. Mom said the potatoes needed to be dug, and the musk and watermelons gathered in. Next to the hog pens, on the side of the hill with sandy soil, was our truck patch. A truck patch was a separate garden where larger items were planted. We had a bumper crop of potatoes and melons. With one horse in a one-shovel plow we plowed the potatoes out, then gathered them and sorted and washed them. Our potato bins in the basement were full, ready for winter. We cleaned up the melons and piled some out by the road with a 'For Sale' sign. We boys took some by horse and buggy to peddle uptown. Mom was great at peddling things.

Once, Dad came home from town with a new John Deere gas engine. We were getting modern! We put a jackshaft in the washhouse with pulleys. We hooked up the engine to pump water and to run the old wood double-tub washer. Now the women did not have to do the washing by hand and we boys did not need to pump water by hand. Whenever the windmill did not run, we had the gas engine to pump water for us. That evening after supper we talked about that new improvement. We thought we were on top of the world. After supper we thanked the Lord for all of his blessings and 'hit the sack'.

In 1930, I was 12 years old. "Today we only need three horses harnessed. Eli, you hitch three horses to the plow and go plow at Plain City near the railroad by the boat factory."

After plowing awhile, I thought the horses needed a rest, so I lay down in the furrow next to the railroad track and took a nap. After I got up and went back to plowing, Johnny Minshall, the Plain City policeman, came out looking around. I stopped and asked what he was looking for. He said, "A train went past and they called back from Milford Center and said a dead man was lying beside the track." I told him I hope he'd find him and went back to plowing. By evening I had plowed about 3 acres.

That same day Ben and Dan took a horse, hitched to a corn sled (cutter), across the road. The horse went between the rows, with a large knife on each side of the corn sled. Straddling the seat, the boys grabbed the cornstalks as they went by. Every 20 feet or so they yelled "Whoa," when they wanted the horse to stop. They got off the seat, carrying armfuls of stalks to make a shock, ran back on the sled and repeated the process all day long. When finished, they went back and tied twine around each shock. By evening the whole field, about 12 or 15 acres, was cut and in shocks, ready for winter. We did not have a corn binder at that time. This took place where the Senior Center is now located.

"Ben, you go out to B.M. Youmans and get a load of cobs." Our washhouse had a two-story adjoining building, where the cobs were put in the top story and the ground floor was filled with wood. We filled the woodhouse with split wood for the cook stove and chunk wood piled to the ceiling for the heating stove. On cold snowy days, all day was spent in the woodhouse, splitting and stacking wood to the ceiling.

"Dan, it is your turn now to split; look how much I did." The cobhouse above had a chute going down, where the cobs would slide to the ground floor. Ben got home with the cobs, they were all unloaded, and we were ready for winter in the woodshed.

This was Saturday and we had one more job, cleaning the chicken houses. We thought we would make this a short job. We started pushing the manure back and brought the straw in right away, keeping the floor covered with straw as we pushed the manure away. We thought we were doing fine, until Mom 'the inspector' came on the scene. "You fellows get all that straw out; you can't fool me. Get all that straw and manure out and scrape those floors, before putting any straw in. Also scrape all the roosts and nests with a knife. No putting straw in 'til I make the final inspection," Mom said. We knew that was final, because outside the house was a tree whose branches were well-trimmed from Mom pulling off little switches. Mom believed in the verse in the Bible that says, "Spare the rod and spoil the child." I thank the Lord for Dad and Mom, who taught us obedience.

Well, the chicken houses were cleaned, and they passed her inspection. Even the chickens seemed to enjoy their clean home. We had one more job to do: jack up the buggy, take the wheels off and grease the hubs, ready for Sunday. Then it was time to get the cows in, do the milking, feed the hogs and the chickens, and put lanterns in the chicken houses. We were all happy with the day's work, even the chickens! The next day was Sunday, and a counsel meeting was scheduled.

On Sundays we got to sleep one half-hour longer, and we ate before chores. We smelled coffee brewing, so we knew it was coffee soup for breakfast. We all helped to milk, but no milk was shipped on Sundays. We had to use a hand-cranked machine to separate the cream from the skim milk. Skim milk was fed to the hogs, and the cream was sold in town the following week.

Dad and Mom left for the counsel meeting, which lasted from 9 a.m. to 4 p.m., discussing church rules and policies. That gave us children a long day to do our own things. We also counseled on things to do. First we had a cat pull. We tied two cats' tails together and watched them pull. Boy, such pulling from each other! It always seemed like the one with the biggest claws had the best footing and was the winner. Next, Dad had a bottle of whiskey in the medicine cabinet for coughs and health aides, and we took a little of the whiskey and gave it to a rooster. The show was on! Such crowing and dancing and spinning around was a sight. Even the chickens watched on!

By then it was noon. The girls were going to make ice cream pudding, so we boys hitched up a cow to the buggy, one boy on each side to guide her, and we went to town to get ice. We ended up in the ditch a few times, but there were very few cars on the road, so we got along pretty good.

We then made the ice cream and had a good feast. By then it was time to clean everything up. Dad and Mom came home about 4:30, and everything looked normal around the farm. Dad thought we were very well-behaved children. It was time for the chores, we had a long Sunday evening, and then we "hit the sack".

On Monday Dad let us have a day of doing things for ourselves. Winter was coming on, so we set our trap lines. Down by the creek we set traps for muskrat, minks, skunks, raccoons, and other furry animals. We also set some traps near a little creek at the back of Burl Mayer's, about a mile to the Cary land and back in the woods. We always checked our trap lines early in the morning, because people would steal animals out of the traps if we waited too late. We had a horse named Sailor that we rode to check the traps.

In the mornings at 5:00, one of us would check our lines. "Look here, fellows, this morning we got two muskrats and one mink!" We took our furs to Red Decker in Plain City. He always treated us good, 35 cents for a rat and $2 for a mink. That would help our budget. Some mornings we got nothing but a foot in the trap; sometimes the animal would chew its foot off and get away. One morning we got a rat with three legs, so we knew we had trapped him before. Sometimes we got a raccoon, which was worth $2 or $3, and sometimes a skunk, which was worth 75 cents.

One time, I went to check the traps and found a funny-looking animal in a trap that snarled and jumped at me. I was afraid and rode home for help. We went back with a rifle and shot it. When we took it to Red, he said, "Boys, you know what you got? That's a red fox." He claimed it was the first one caught around there and gave us $4 for it. But as we were getting only $1.50 a month from Dad, those fur prices were a big help to buy candy, gum, and other things we didn't need.

Once we caught a skunk. We purposely got a little careless and let it perfume us a little, because when we went to school, the teacher sent us home.

Being that the fall and winter were coming on, it was time for butchering. I was given the job of letting folks know, either by horseback or bicycle, or maybe a one-cent postcard. Word went out to about eight families. Thursday was butchering day at the Helmuth farm.

Up early, chores done, and large iron kettles, maybe 5 or 6 of them, were filled with water. The kettles were in iron jackets, and fires built under them. People started arriving at seven, and by then the water was boiling hot.

The hogs had been penned up for slaughter, and men went to the hog pens with rifles and knives. Two hogs were shot, and one man ran up with a knife and stuck a hog in the throat, so as to bleed it. Then the hog was put on a sled and pulled to the barnyard for scalding. The big scalding tank was there with hot water, and the hog was put in and rolled back and forth. Then it was rolled out onto the platform and men with scrapers in hand scraped all the hair off, then hung the hog on a scaffold, head down. They slit it open, and all the insides were taken out. The head was cut off, and then the hog was cut in two pieces. It was carried to the washhouse where the women cut it up, taking the intestines outside on a table, cleaning and scraping them. The men outside continued with each hog, until all eight were finished, usually by 11:00 in the morning. Then the processing began.

There were four hams on each hog. All the skins were cut in pieces, ready for the lard press. The sausage was ground up and put through the sausage stuffer into the intestine skins, ready for the smokehouse. The hams were trimmed up, nice and ready for the smokehouse too.

The smokehouse was behind the barn, down at the end of the hill. A fire was built and sawdust put on the fire. The hams were smoked for a week or so. Then they were put in the basement for storage. That was good for the winter!

The heads of the hogs were cut up, and also the liver was ground, mixed with head cheese, making the liverwurst. The hides of the hogs, all cut into little pieces, were cooked and then put through a lard press. Lard was put in five-gallon lard cans.

When all this was finished and the cleaning done, it was 5:00 in the afternoon. The whole gang gathered around and had a real feast. All left for home, and we did the chores. The basement was now loaded with meat, the smokehouse was full, and we had 8 less hogs to feed. The next day was peddling day.

Mom was great for sending us out to do peddling. We put a big cooker, full of sausage and ham and other meats, on the buggy. Dan and I were to be the salesmen.

Mom said, "Go uptown to Joe Hofbauer at the meat market and ask for the prices, then sell the meat for a few cents less." Well, we thought that was foolish, so we just decided on a price and started at the south edge of town. We'd take turns going in.

The first house was Charles Lowry's. "Yes, we will take some." Next was Rodney Bidwell's, who also wanted some. Next was Charlie Grubb's, then Ed Gannon's, and they both wanted some. By the time we got to town, the meat was all sold. Now that was unusual, so we decided to go to the meat market and ask about the prices. Here we had been selling the meat for half price! Now we were in deep trouble.

On the way home Dan and I debated what to do. We dared not lie or we would really be in trouble. So we decided to be honest and tell Mom just how it was, and we would plead for mercy. When we got home, we gave Mom the money and said we were sorry. She accepted our confession, and we promised that it would not happen again.

Another time, we had a roaster full of meat, when we hit a little dip in the road. The roaster slid off onto the road, scattering meat everywhere. We gathered it all up, washed the meat, and continued down the road, selling.

One time on butchering day, the milkman stopped to pick up the milk, and we boys tied hogs' tails to the back of his truck. He drove off. He had the tails, and we had the heads.

We boys were allowed to do odd jobs to earn a little money. We trimmed around gravestones at Forest Grove Cemetery, one cent for each gravestone. Sometimes we would go pigeon-catching, climbing up in high barns with flashlights. I think we got 15 cents each. As I remember, sometimes we would catch 25 or 30 pigeons in one night, but had to divide the money among four boys.

Once, I sent for 12 jars of Rosebud Salve to sell. I went on the road with my bike to sell them for 25 cents each, and then I could pick a gift from their catalogue. One time I got a BB gun. Dad didn't like that, but I did because I could shoot at the sparrows.

Easter Monday was a day that some people worked, but others didn't. Dad let me take two horses and a wagon with a walking plow, and go uptown to plow gardens. I would get from $1 to $2 a garden. The next-door neighbor came over once and wanted his garden plowed. I made about $10 that day. I was rich!

But the next day was sad. When doing my trap lines I saw that someone had stolen all of my traps. So I had to send to Sears for traps, and that took about all of the money I had earned, so I was poor again. Oh, well, I figured that I would make it up somehow again.

A winter in the woods on the Cary land. With a two-man cross-cut saw, axe, sledge and chisel, all the cutting-down of trees and sawing them up for firewood was done by hand. We didn't have any chain saws.

We felled a tree, cutting it in pieces ready for the stove. If snow was on the ground, the wood was hauled home by a sled. If not, then a wagon was used. A few times when a tree was felled, raccoons came out of their home in the tree. That made us a little money, as we would get three or four dollars for them. This wood-cutting lasted all winter. But that was our only way of heating and cooking for the home. In later years Dad did buy some coal.

Another winter job was to haul manure and clean out the loafing shed and the box stalls. Two or three of us would load the manure spreader; one would take it out to the field, and we would trade off. There was no manure loader on the Helmuth farm; we had to do it all by hand. We always bedded the barn down with straw; the cows loved that.

My Dad had an agreement with our neighbor, Walter Navin, to keep his barn cleaned out. We hauled the manure home, for the manure. We boys did not think that was a good deal, but Dad did. The distance was about a mile.

Christmas at the Helmuth home. Peeking down through the register, trying to see anything going on, but all was quiet. The roosters crowed, and Dad said it was time to get up. Coffee soup for breakfast, then all out to do the milking and chores. No horses to get ready, just milking and feeding the chickens, hogs, and calves. Snow on the ground, no Christmas trees or Santa Claus or lights, just oil lanterns and lamps. After all the chores were done, all to the house we go, to relax and spend the day loafing.

The first thing on the agenda: we all had to take a large spoonful of castor oil before the goodies were eaten. No castor oil, no candy. But then, before the candy and presents, we all had to sit quietly while Dad read the Christmas story and told about the birth of Christ, telling what Christmas was all about. Then Mom went to the closet and got some candy, oranges and other goodies. She also got some small gifts, like crayons, coloring books, pencils, handkerchiefs, and other items. We could eat candy and play with our gifts, and then at noon we had a big meal: mashed potatoes, gravy, chicken, dressing, pie and a lot of other goodies.

In the afternoon everyone was free to do whatever they wanted to do. We had neighbors, Tom and Bill Bowman, across the railroad tracks behind our farm. They had a little brown dog named Brownie that could outrun any rabbit. We boys and they would go out rabbit-hunting. We'd get on top of the brush piles and stomp the rabbits out. Then the run was on, and we would sometimes end up with six or eight rabbits. We divided them and would have rabbit meat for a few days for dinner.

Two weeks after Christmas was Old Christmas, on January 6th. Some people observed it as a very holy day. We did not work on that day. There was an old wives' fable that if you go to the barn at midnight and talk to the cows, they would talk back. We never dared do it; we did not want back-talk from a cow, I guess.

After the chores in the evening, again we had a big supper. Maybe strawberry shortcake and homemade ice cream. We had lots of fun after supper, playing games, reading, singing and story-telling. "Eli, it's your turn to go out and shut the windmill off." Then to bed on our straw-filled mattresses, no innersprings.

Now to some of my school days' experiences. Mom made me a new pair of pants, a shirt made from 'Wayne' feed sacks and a pair of rubber suspenders made from a rubber innertube. Off to school. The school bus was an old Model T Ford, about a 1924 model. Sometimes it would get stuck, as the road past our house was still not graveled. I could say only a few words in English. My first few years were spent playing marbles at recess time and learning to speak English.

In about the fifth grade things changed, and I was getting away from my Amish shyness. Now my teacher was Mrs. Toops. On the school bus I would try to sit beside one of the Torbert girls, who were not Amish. They were neighbors of ours.

In sixth grade, a certain girl called me "Amish," so I called her "Nigger." She hit me on the head with a book, and Mrs. Scott sent us to the office, where Mr. Gower was the superintendent. He was a big man, and said, "What's the problem?"

The girl said, "Eli called me Nigger," and I said, "Well, she called me Amish."

Mr. Gower said, "That's what you are, ain't you?" We were both sentenced to the paddle. Of course, I didn't tell about it at home because I knew it would be the paddle there too.

In the fall and spring of that year I had to stay at home for about two days each week to work. The teacher would send home a report card asking about the absence, and Dad would just write on it 'Work'. As I got older and taller I was always picked first to play volleyball. I was popular also in other ball games because of my height and strength. One time, I was playing ball and slid into first base. Being a bleeder, I was laid up for three weeks. I didn't play ball after that.

I only went through eighth grade. In those days that was all that was required. So at 13 years of age I graduated from school. My eight years were at the Plain City School. Christian schools were unheard of then. I asked Mrs. Ero Scott, one of my teachers, why there were no school pictures of me. She said, "Eli, you know why. You were always absent when pictures were taken."

Some of my close friends were: Warren Moore, who lived on West Ave. in Plain City; Virginia Torbert lived on the Torbert farm, where Roger and Sue Hostetler now live; Wanda Torbert, later Mrs. Joe Rummell of Rummell Insurance; and Edith Fitzgerald, now a Sister in the Catholic church. I have many fond memories of those school days. Oh, yes, we walked down to Della Trees' for crayons and school items. She had a little store at the corner of Bigelow Ave. and Maple St.

It was now spring of 1931. Most of the plowing was done in the fall, but there were still a few fields to plow before spring planting. So after our regular routine of chores, three of us boys would take one five-horse team with a gang plow and a two to three-horse team with a one-bottom plow. We could plow seven or eight acres a day.

While we let the horses rest at the back end of the field by the train tracks, we would put nails on the tracks. After the train went by we would hunt for our nails, flattened to all kinds of shapes. It was interesting to see the figures they were in.

After days of plowing fields, it was oat-sowing time. A four-horse team in the disc, a four-horse team in the harrow, and a three-horse team in the grain drill. We could do about ten acres a day.

Next was corn-planting time with the same outfits, except the drill was replaced with a corn planter with two horses. Before we went to the field we picked out corn from the crib, shelled the corn in a hand corn-sheller, separating the corn from the cobs. Then we used a hand-grader, shaking the small kernels from the large. No hybrid corn in those days.

The corn and fertilizer were hauled to the field; the fertilizer came in 125-pound bags then. The planter had corn bins and fertilizer bins that were filled.

The first thing with the planter was to unroll wire the whole length of the field. The wire had knots every forty inches, and there was a stake at each end of the field. Then the planter was lined up in a straight line with the wires. The planter had an arm out the side. As we made for a straight line down the field, the planter dropped two kernels at each click at the knot on the wire. Going click, click, click, and so on.

At the end, the wire was released and the planter turned around. The stake was moved with the wire over to line up with the planter again. We tried to pull the wire with the same tension, so as to make the drops line up across the field. That was a contest, so to speak, in the community, to see who could have the straightest row each way. We also cultivated the corn crossways after it was up and growing. I remember we boys taking pride in having straight rows each way. We could plant about five acres a day.

After the corn was up and about four inches tall, we had three single-row cultivators, two horses for each. We had now advanced from walking cultivators to the riding type.

After the corn had been gone over once, it was hay-making time. I was uptown mowing, where the Senior Center now is, and had a new John Deere mower with a six-foot cutting bar. The flies were bad, and one of the horses got its bridle caught under the neck yoke, and I could not control them. They ran for home through the town streets, but the only car that was hit was Walter Mooney's car. The mower broke in two pieces and the horses ran on home. Dad had to pay for the car damage, and he also bought a new mower. As I remember, the mower cost $85. I don't remember what the car damage cost. Lawsuits were unheard of then.

After the hay was mowed, it cured for about two or three days, and then a side-delivery rake was used to rake the hay in rows. The wagon had a seat on the front for the driver. Three slings, which were wood slats running crosswise, were on the wagon. One sling was spread on the wagon floor with the hay loader behind the wagon. The driver straddled the rows, and two of us were on the wagon. The hay came up the loader onto the wagon, and we put the hay in place, trying to make a very nice load. When there were about two feet of hay on the wagon, another sling was spread over the hay. Then on the go again, spreading the hay over the next sling.

"Jonas, shloh nunnah. Kumm naett so shteik." (Slow those horses down a little; you're coming too fast)

After the loading was completed with a nice rounded load about eight feet high, the loader was unhooked, and we set off for the barn. The large barn had a gable extended out at the roof. Two horses were ready to pull the slingful up to the barn track and into the haymow. When Dad yelled, we tripped the sling and the hay dropped down to the mow. Dad and one of us boys were usually up in the mow. We sometimes had them about covered up. Sometimes one of us boys would ride the loaded sling up and then be dropped off up in the mow. We did, on average, ten or twelve loads a day. That was a dirty, dusty day. After the day was finished and the chores were all done, we took off for the creek, down at the end of our pasture, for a swim in the nudist bath hole. Now that was quite a treat!

By then it was time to cultivate the corn the second time, and this time it was crossways. Dad complimented us for the straight rows crossways. We really did appreciate that Dad complimented us for a good job.

After the cornfields were all taken care of the second time, it was time for the wheat and oats harvest. We got the grain binder out and greased it all up, and then got the canvasses, by which we elevated the grain to the knotter, where it was tied in sheaves. Four horses pulled the binder. As the binder went through the field, it tied the grain in sheaves, and they were dropped maybe 25 feet apart. Dad usually ran the machine and we boys did the shocking. About six or seven sheaves stood together with a cap on top. Again, we tried to see who could make the nicest shocks and the straightest rows.

At one time, we had two boys from town to help shock. They were Jim Srapp and Lester Evans. We boys had fun trying to teach them Pennsylvania Dutch! One time we told one to ask my sister Fannie, "Gleichsht du mich?" (Do you like me?) We had a lot of fun with those boys. Later, Jim was in the dry-cleaning business and Lester had a little store on U.S. Rt. 42 at the north edge of Plain City. I met his daughter a few years ago at the Plain City Auction. She said, "You are the guy that tried to teach my dad Dutch!" We had a good time discussing those days.

After all the grain was cut and in shocks, it was time for the third round of cultivating the corn, which was called "laying by." No sprays those days. Then it was time for the threshing. My Dad, Levi Hostetler, and Jonas Gingerich bought a new Red River threshing machine and a new John Deere tractor.

Our threshing ring consisted of about eight or ten families, and we took turns as to where to thresh. About 6 rack wagons and two box grain wagons were used, and four men were pitchers in the field. They pitched the sheaves to the guys on the wagons, who made a nice load, again seeing who could make the nicest loads. There was usually a good discussion between the pitcher and the loader.

The threshing machine was backed to the barn with the straw blower stuck in the straw shed. The tractor lined up to the large belt, one wagon load on each side, and the grain wagon under the grain spout to catch the grain. The machine was started and the sheaves from the wagons were pitched in. The grain came out of the threshing machine in half-bushel dumps. There was one man up in the straw shed with a handkerchief around his neck and goggles on, because it was very dusty up there.

Many times I had the job of hauling the grain away, sometimes to town to the grain elevator, either to B.M. Youmans or to Nau Grain Co. Many times I was gone to town over lunch time and got home after the men had finished eating and were back to work. I had to go in and eat with the women. Oh, that was such a hard thing to do; I was so bashful that I sometimes cried. But it had to be that way, because I was too little to pitch or haul in from the field.

Many times we threshed very late. The women did the chores and the milking. After a big day we went home, unhitching the horses and feeding them. With our clothes all dusty, it was time to go for the creek, throw off our clothes, shake the dust off, and hit the nudist swimming hole.

Now to the oats-threshing. The oats were pulled up into the grainery with a big round tank. No elevators or motors then, all done by hand with the horses pulling.

A few weeks after the oats and wheat threshing were over, a threshers' meeting was called. All the bushels had been recorded and the time spent at each farm. At the meeting, all was figured up, how many bushels each one had, how many hours and the number of persons involved; each was paid according to what he had. Then the ice cream and cake were served.

One time, we were threshing at Charlie Roby's, and he wanted to use his steam engine for the power. That was interesting, to hear the puffing and smoking; it was fired up by wood in the engine. Charlie let me drive his 1930-model truck with the grain. Boy, talk about a proud Amish boy!

A few months after the grain harvest, it was silo-filling time. Corn was cut by a corn binder, and the silo filler was set up with long pipes up to the top of the silo and down inside. Two or three wagons were used to haul cornstalks. We fed the cornstalks into the corn cutter, which then blew it into the silo. Two men in the silo spread and stomped it down. One silo was filled in a day.

It was now time to start husking corn. Some were put in shocks, and some husked right from the stalk. The corn in shocks was laid on the ground and husked in piles on the ground.

Sometimes a "bashting" (husking) was made for the young people. Maybe 25 or 30 people were invited in for a bashting. Boys would pick a girl to husk with, a boy on one side and a girl on the other side, hoping to find a red ear of corn, which meant a kiss. After three or four hours of husking, they all got together at the house for some treats and games. Sometimes we boys took our partners home and spent a few hours visiting.

Now for husking the stalks in the field. Four wagons were pulled by two horses each, with two of us at each wagon. Straddling the rows, each wagon took three rows; that's 12 rows as we went. The wagons had high boards along one side, and we pitched the ears as we went. The girls helped with a peg in their right hands, husking by hand. Again, we prided ourselves in trying to husk the ears clean.

Then, off to the barn, with each having a load of maybe 50 bushels in each wagon. Unloading was all done by hand with a scoop shovel, no elevators on this farm. A good meal at noon, then back to the field again. Husking lasted three to four weeks. The cribs were full of nice yellow corn, ready for winter.

The hay was in the barn, the grain in the bin, the silo full, and the corn in the crib. The woodshed was full of wood, the cobhouse full of cobs, and all was ready now for a cold winter.

It was now wedding time. On one Sunday at church, Preacher Jake Farmwald announced the up-coming marriage of Freeman Detweiler and Martha Helmuth. Freeman was from Oklahoma and Martha was my sister. In ten days, on a Thursday, would be the big day! For the next ten days, friends and relatives got together to shine the cookware and dishes, butcher 50 to 60 chickens, peal bushels of potatoes, make bread, apple butter, peanut butter, and bake many cakes, especially the big cake.

The house was all cleaned, also the barn. People were invited by horseback, bike, and one-cent post cards. We boys went after the bench wagon, which belonged to the church. The benches were all arranged, two benches side by side, then a bench on each side to sit on. These were set up all through the house. In the main room they were set up in an "L" shape. The "Ekk" (corner table where the couple sat) was set up with a large decorated cake. The church wedding started at nine in the morning. The couple had picked two other couples to be "nayva hokkah", a best girl and boy.

After the preaching, prayers, and singing, the Bishop asked the couple, are they still agreed to be united. Then he gave the vows. After dismissal, all went to the house, where the tables were set up (the services were held in a neighbor's house). All were seated according to relatives. The couple sat in the "Ekk" and their "nayva hokkah" on each side. Oh yes, Freeman's "nayva hokkah" were Joni Yoder and Barbara Detweiler, Freeman's sister; Martha's "nayva hokkah" were Dan Helmuth, our brother, and Edna Yutzy. Eight or ten couples had been chosen for table waiters, usually relatives or close friends. Grace was said, and then the big feast was on. Such a feast!

Supper was also served at five or six in the evening. Some went home to do the chores and then came back around 7 p.m. The young folks picked partners to eat with. All of a sudden there was a rattling of pans and a gunshot outside the window! Oh, the bellers had arrived - some who maybe thought they should have been invited but weren't. Dad took some food out to them and tried to calm them down, but they were not let in the house. Sometimes they accepted that; other times they got a little unruly. The wedding usually lasted till midnight or even later.

After the wedding day was over, it usually took a few days to get back to normal. No honeymoons in those days, other than sitting out in the yard during a full moon, enjoying each other, or out in the wheat field, shocking wheat under a full moon.

It was getting toward spring, time to get the brooder house ready for chicks. The brooder house was cleaned, and a little stove put in that burns charcoal. Eggs were put in a wood incubator with an oil lamp on the end of the incubator, which kept the temperature even. The eggs were turned every day, and in three weeks we would start hearing the chicks chirp. In a few days they were taken out and put in the brooder house. They would huddle together at night by the little stove. When we opened the door to feed them, they scampered away, chirping. It was a beautiful sight.

Some mother hens would choose to do their own brooding. They would lay eggs in the barn in some hidden place, sit on them for three weeks, and then come out in the open, strutting around with their new chick family, proud as can be. And you'd better not try to touch the chicks, as the mother would take after you. Other spring jobs were to round up all the lambs and cut their tails off, and to dehorn the cattle that had horns.

We had a team of horses that could outpull any horses in the area. Many of the neighbors borrowed them to move brooder houses. They were a light orange color, named Nick and Dick. The road past our house was still gravel, so a lot of gravel was hauled in to fill holes. One time we were hauling gravel from our neighbor Dan Hostetler's gravel pit. Dan was gone from home and his son Abe took care of the pit. We boys had always thought we had the best horses. We had a load of gravel and Abe said, "I know your horses can't pull that out. I'll hook my team on and pull it out for you."

Dad said, "Abe, I'll pull that out with one horse." Abe laughed and said that if we could pull it out with one horse, he'd *give* us the gravel. Dad unhitched the one horse, said "Giddap, Dick," and away we went. Down the road we went with that load of gravel. Abe had a problem with what his Dad would say when he got home. The end of the story is that Dad did not accept the load of gravel free.

Some springs, when we got loads of rain, our creek bottom overflowed. The whole bottom land was under water, sometimes hip-deep. All kinds of fish came in with the water. When the water started to go down, the fish didn't leave soon enough. Then we rolled our pants' legs up and got the fish; sometimes we got as many as a hundred fish, mostly carp. Some were the size of a little coaster wagon. We fed many to the hogs and gave others away. Usually, the water stayed in the bottom for four or five days. Of course, after the water went down, we had fences to fix, as all kinds of tree limbs came down the creek, tearing fences out.

Spring was also a time for plowing the garden. After plowing the ground, it was raked and leveled. A path was shoveled out about two feet wide and six inches deep all around the garden, and also two or three paths through the garden. We had to lay boards on the soil, so as not to make foot prints. Mom and the girls did the planting, and they always had a beautiful garden with lots of flowers. It was always a beautiful sight, and people would drive by and look at it.

Another job, about every two years, we did not care to do – cleaning the outhouse, or backhouse as it was called. There were eleven of us in the family who occupied it at different times, plus about five or six Sears catalogues.

The outhouse had two holes that we moved off the platform. We had to put hankies over our noses because the smell was almost unbearable. We used a mud boat, as it was called, which is like a sled with straw on the bottom. We scooped the contents onto the sled and hauled it to the field, and spread it. Boy, that made for good fertilizer. By the way, whenever someone was missing from the house, they would many times be out in the backhouse, looking at the Sears catalogue.

"Boys, get all the sheep into the barn, as Eli Troyer is coming to shear them." Eli pulled into the lane with a horse and small trailer behind a buggy, with a clipping machine and gas engine on the cart. Eli could shear maybe 30 or 40 sheep in a few hours. He would tie up the wool of each sheep in a bundle, and put the bundles on a pile. In a few days someone would come by to pick it up, or sometimes we hauled it to Fee Brothers in Plain City. Sometimes the sheep would run and shiver, as it was a little cool yet.

One day, Dan and I were coming home from hauling manure at Walter Navin's. Dan was driving and I was sitting on the side, when the spreader flew into gear, and caught my leg, tearing a big gash in my leg under the knee. Being a bleeder, I bled profusely. Hospitals were pretty much a 'No' to us, so they wrapped my leg and put me in bed. Blood soon seeped through the bandages, so they wrapped it again, but it kept on bleeding. There was blood all over the bed and the floor. I must have passed into a coma. When I regained consciousness, the whole family was standing around the bed, crying. I guess they thought that was the end of my life. But then they decided to take me to the hospital to sew up the big gash. This was during the depression years, and in the hospital we went to a department where service was free. I still have a large mark on my leg where this happened.

This was my third bleeding experience, and I would have many more through the years. I was 13 years old at this time. After this experience, my parents started taking me to the hospital to get wounds and cuts stitched up.

We had about 20 horses in all, with some nice sorrel mares. We had about four colts every year. By now we had advanced from two-horse buggy hitches to one-horse, as the roads were not mud roads anymore. Thereby, we had double-driving harnesses that we no longer used. So when the colts were about three or four months old, we boys cut the double-driving harnesses down to small colts' sizes and trained the colts to be hitched. We had them trained real well and hitched them up to the coaster wagon. Boy, that was a beautiful sight.

Rodney Bidwell and Henry Conklin were horse dealers. They would stop to take pictures and wanted to take them to the fair, but Dad said no. Oh, what I would give for some of those pictures. But Dad said he would not permit us to train colts like that anymore because when they were older and we used them in the field, they were more like pets and very stubborn.

One time, we had them hitched to the little wagon, and they started running. As they ran, the tongue of the wagon hit their feet and so they ran faster. Finally the wagon flew off and tore off into the ditch. The colts ran down the road to their mothers, hitched to a wagon at Al Miller's. They ran up to their mothers and started nursing from them.

By now, we had advanced on the farm from oil lanterns and lamps to gas lanterns and lamps. From sad irons that were heated on top of the stove, to gas irons. The big change came when we put in a bathroom. We had a stool and bathtub, but no water heater. We heated a kettle full of water, then poured it into the tub to make the water lukewarm. We put a water tank up in the attic. The water was pumped into the tank by a windmill. It would take up most of a Saturday afternoon for all the family to bathe. We also advanced to a wooden icebox, the top holding 50 pounds of ice. The iceman came one or two times a week. We had a cord with a sign which we hung in the window, telling how much ice we needed.

Another project my mother had going on was ordering barrels full of cups and saucers, plates, soup plates, and all kinds of dishes. We boys were given the job of loading the buggy with dishes and going out to peddle them. We were the salesmen. Maybe that is why I became an auction house owner and salesman in later years. I was now 14 years old, and I had graduated from the eighth grade. Now I was a full-time farmer and peddler.

When I graduated, the teacher gave each of us a cracker. When we started to eat our crackers, the one who ate the cracker and whistled first was the winner. I won, and I got a jar of red heart candy. Also, the one to memorize the Gettysburg Address the best was the winner, and I was also the winner of that. Not bad for an Amish boy!

Now that I was 14 and Ben was getting a little older, we boys were hired out sometimes. I worked for a young couple that had just married. They did a lot of fussing and arguing, and I thought I never wanted to get married. The next two years I worked for Ray Miller, John Lapp, and others. Later, I worked for Al Miller. He had a great family, and they had devotions every morning. He was such a good influence on me that I thought, oh yes, I do want to get married. It was such a pleasure working there.

From ages 15 to 16, we boys worked at a lot of different places. One job I had was working at the canning factory, where sweet corn was processed. Feeding corn into the husking bed was a man's job. My buddy said I should chew tobacco because it would make time go fast. So I went uptown and got some chewing tobacco. And I got sick, I mean sick. That was the end of my tobacco-chewing.

At 16, Dad gave me a horse and buggy. Boy, that was like owning a Cadillac. Decorated and shined up, it had rings and loops, and red tassels on the side of the bridle. I had the prettiest rig in the Plain City area. I didn't know what pride was then, but my rig was the best, and I am sure that even the girls knew who owned that outfit.

The Helmuth farm could have been called "Helmuth Brothers Circus" because we had trained a lot of the animals to perform. When we let the cows out of the stalls, we would jump on one of their backs and ride along out, several times failing to stoop down at the doorway. That meant a bump on the head. We were sorry when the cows were dehorned, because it did not give us horns to hold onto. The sheep buck was also a good one to ride. We had the buck come toward us, trying to ram us. Then we'd jump away, which made him mad. Also, we liked to ride a few of the bigger hogs. Another thing we did was throw a cat on the tin roof of the large barn, watching it slide down. I guess you could call that a cat-sliding board.

As I was now 16 and had a horse and buggy of my own, I took great pride in keeping the outfit shined up, with a nice horse-hide robe for winter and a fancy duster for summer. It was customary then to go to Plain City every Saturday evening; the young people would gather at George Elias' ice cream store. Cones were 5 cents. We also went to a few restaurants where we could get sandwhiches for 5 to 10 cents and milkshakes for 15 cents. We usually got back home at midnight.

There were three Amish churches in the area, South Church and East Church on the same Sunday, and the West Church on the opposite Sunday. No Sunday schools were held then, and church was every other Sunday. But every Sunday evening there was a young people's "Singing". Singing was in German, with a few English songs. It was the custom then after Singing for a young man to have someone else ask a girl for a date.

When word got around that certain parents would be gone from their home, a crowd was announced to be at that house in the evening. Games were played, the harp and accordian were played, and we would have a real Amish hodown. We picked a girl to take home. In the winter, the young folks would come together to do ice skating at our house, because we had a large pond down in our pasture field. We also went sledding down the hill onto the pond.

One evening I was at a party at Eli Frey's. I saw a pretty girl standing on the other side of the room, but I was too shy to talk to her. Later at another place I saw that same girl, and she looked prettier than the time before. But no way did I have enough nerve to talk to her. I just kept eyeing her each time I saw her. I was still too bashful to get close. After I was 17, I got someone else to ask her for a date, and she accepted. On the way to take her home, very few words were spoken, as I was extremely shy.

But after about six months we were going steady. Her name was Martha Miller, daughter of Preacher one-armed Joe Miller. Her home was eight miles from mine, and that was a long way for my horse. My mother told me one day, "If you can get Joe Miller's daughter, you are lucky." She has now been my wife for 65 years.

On one occasion on the way to see her, my good horse fell over and died, right on the road in front of where Johnny Yoder now lives. Dad got me another good horse. In later years I told Martha that, not only did Christ give His life for her, but my horse also did. Rumors were then just like they are now. Many rumors circulated about my horse's death. In those days, boys would come to Plain City from out west to work in the area. Sometimes another boy would get himself a date and we would go on what they called a double date. Sam Petersheim was dating Barbara Detweiler, and we four would go in one buggy, each holding his partner in his lap.

On another occasion, John Gingerich went with me. I had a date with Martha, and John had a date with Edna Miller. The girls were neighbors. Later that night I went home and forgot about John. I didn't think about it until the next day in the field. John had to walk home eight miles. John assured me before he died that he had forgiven me.

Sometimes I would send a one-cent postcard to Martha, asking her to come to town on Saturday night with Alvin Plank, a neighbor. There was no phone service those days. Sometimes leaving the Miller home, I would throw the lines over the dashboard of the buggy and take a nap. The horse knew the way home.

Once I sent to Sears for a new lapel suit and a necktie. I think it was about $4.95 for the suit and 19 cents for the tie. We had a half mile to our mailbox at the end of the road, and orders from Sears always came in three days. So on the third day I was sure to go to the mailbox. The box was there and I took it home and hid it. On a certain night I got all dressed up in my new outfit. I stood in front of the mirror and thought I looked like a Boston lawyer. I took off to see Martha, thinking, "She will be proud of me." But no way. She did not like it at all. I thought, boy, I made a mistake. She was more important to me than the suit and necktie, so I went home, wrapped them up, and sent them back to Sears. They sent me my money back (Satisfactory or your money back), because it sure wasn't satisfactory to Martha. I have never had a tie on since, and still have Martha. Praise the Lord.

One evening I thought I would go on the bike to see Martha. We did have a bike at that time. I came home about midnight, put my bike out by the barn, climbed up on the milkhouse and from there to the washhouse, and then onto the porch roof. All of them were connected. Jonas was in bed inside the window. The noise woke him up and off he took for downstairs, telling Mom and Dad that someone climbed up on the roof, ready to come in the window. "Oh, Jonas, you are day-dreaming." By that time I was in bed. My parents came upstairs and I was make-believe snoring. So they let Jonas sleep with them. The next morning at the breakfast table they talked about that episode. I guess the thought was that Jonas was dreaming.

2

My Sweetheart

Early Married Life

My allowance was still $1.50 a month, but I could make some money by trapping, and Dad would let me have a few days each year to plow some gardens. I also did some odd jobs in the evenings, like trimming around tombstones at the graveyard. So I did have a few dollars to get married on December 10, 1936, to Martha, my wife now of 65 years. No honeymoon in those days. I guess we are still honeymooning after 65 years. Dad gave me a horse and buggy, a team of horses, one cow, and a desk. Martha's parents gave us a bureau, cupboard, and a bedroom suite. We were close to 19 years old at the time.

Preacher Al Miller came to us, offering to lend us money, interest-free, to help us buy machinery and implements, if we wanted to start farming. We rented a farm one-half mile south of Plain City, owned by Dr. Eli Holmes. It had 83 acres for $450 cash rent, annually. The land was very poor, and so were we. The farmhouse had no modern conveniences, no electricity, and no phone. Martha did the clothes-washing with a hand washer for the first year. We had an old-fashioned wood cook stove and a coal-heating stove.

We raised some chickens and had about 7 or 8 cows. The farming was done with horses. We had to have the milk ready for the milkman by 6:25 a.m. That meant early rising. Sometimes I would walk to town with a chicken or two to sell, in order to buy groceries. There was a store in a house about a half mile away, and I took eggs and traded them for groceries. It was closer than the back of our pasture, so I walked instead of going to get the horse. We could not pay the rent, so Dad signed a note for us to borrow the money. That's the way it was for about 3 or 4 years. Deeper and deeper in debt. But Dad said farming was the only way for us as Amish.

As we had not been members of the Amish Church, we were under instruction and then were baptized and taken into the Amish Church. It was not the custom to join the Church and be baptized until about age 20.

MARTHA:

Our first daughter was born in 1937. Louella was her name. Louella got sick with a bad skin problem called impetigo. She was sick for about six weeks. Dr. Henry Karrer from Dublin would come out every morning to treat her. The scabs would have to be picked off before salve was put on. Then she got a bad cold, and the infection got into her blood. She died then, at 7 months of age. She was such a beautiful baby. We never gave it a thought that we could lose her.

Jacob Freeman was born in 1938. He was called Jakie. When women were pregnant, for four months before the date of birth, they would stay at home. People would say, "Did you know Martha Helmuth is staying home?" After the birth of the child, she would stay in bed for nine days. A hired girl would work for us, for $3 to $4 a week.

When Jakie was born, I nursed him, but he didn't seem to gain as he should. My mother said, "Yes, the frame is growing, but he's not filling out." So we put him on a bottle, and he gained from then on. I would make cow's milk boiling hot, then strain it into bottles, and add one tablespoon Karo to each bottle. Jakie was a very contented and good baby. He was slow in the beginning to walk and talk.

When Jakie was 6-7 months old, I was invited to a quilting at my Aunt Susie's, Mrs. Mose H. Kaufman. We had a new driving horse, and about halfway there the horse started to run. He put the bit in his teeth and went for it. I pulled on the reins with all my might. Jakie slid down between my legs and I braced my feet against the dashboard. I was afraid the wheels would fly apart. Finally, at Dan Stutzman's, where Ray Stutzmans now live, I turned in and got the horse stopped. The horse and I both panted and relaxed for awhile. I went on, and he ran normally from then on. When I got to Susie's I called Eli and said to come get me in the evening. An English (non-Amish) neighbor took me home, and Eli drove the rig. When he came home he said, "Am I ever glad you didn't try to drive home." That was the end of having that horse.

At that time, Martha got a gasoline-powered wringer clothes washer. In 1938 the Amish Church started to allow tractors. I had bought a cow from my sister Emma for $25. I had no money, but gave her a promise note. I traded the cow in as a down-payment for a used John Deere tractor. I could not meet the payments, so the finance company took the tractor back. Then I did not have a tractor or a cow and still owed Emma for the cow. For the next two years I farmed with horses again.

In 1939, we had another baby boy, delivered by Dr. Holmes, costing $20. William, or Willie as we called him, was born the morning the corn shredders gang was coming for lunch. I don't remember how it all went. I suppose some women came and helped, and we would have had a hired girl, only I don't remember who. Willie nearly caught up with Jakie, and they started talking at about the same time. Throughout their growing-up years, they wore the same size clothes.

We had payments to make at Sears and Penney's that were hard to meet. We had debts in many places; even some of the baby deliveries weren't paid yet. In 1941 my Dad bought a farm, where Frieda Whitmer now lives, close to Amlin. Dad bought that farm of 100 acres for $10,000, at $1,000 a year for 10 years.

We moved there and farmed 50/50. It was about 12 miles from Martha's parents' place, which was quite a distance with horse and buggy. We had no phone or electricity. We were still husking all the corn by hand. The farm had good black soil, and we could raise good crops. We raised corn, oats, wheat, hay, and sweet corn that was hauled and sold to the canning factory in Plain City, where the boat factory is now located. I did a lot of corn-husking for neighbors at ten cents a bushel. I would husk 100 bushels a day, and also did a lot of custom plowing around Amlin with my tractor. Dan Yutzy worked for me at this time. He told me later that he thought he was the fastest worker but was humiliated when Martha could outdo him in pulling sweet corn.

My brother Jonas was helping me husk corn one day. He said, "I'll tell you something if you don't tell anyone I told you."

"Okay," I said.

He said, "Tomorrow in church our sister Emma (then age 40) is to be published," meaning an announcement would be made that she was to get married.

"What? To whom?"

He said to Al Yoder, a widower. Not knowing she ever had a date, talk about a surprise. That evening while milking, I told Martha to sit down, I'd tell her a surprise, and she said she could take anything standing. When I told her, she almost went down. We did not go to church the next day, because we could not face it. In those days romances were kept very secret.

MARTHA:

Carolyn was born in 1941. She was past due, so Dr. Herman Karrer decided to induce labor. Well, nothing happened, so they took me to the hospital and shortly after we got there, Carolyn was born. She was a lot more feisty than Jakie or Willie. They used to say you shouldn't spank a child before it's a year old, and I wondered what you would want to spank it for. Well, Carolyn at six months would stiffen herself and get mad, and that called for a light swat. I firmly believe that teaching a child to be submissive to authority is one of the most important lessons to teach.

Elizabeth was born in 1942. We called her Betty. When she was born, she was quite jaundiced. She was a fussy baby and didn't do well at first. We finally got goat's milk for her, and that was better.

We had some interesting experiences when we lived on that farm. In the old brick house, a front window had a hole in the glass about six inches round. One evening after coming home from town, we put the groceries on the table, including a loaf of bread. We went out to do the milking. After milking, when we came back to the house, the rats had carried all the bread from the wrapper, and the wrapper stood there so nice, but not a crumb of bread was left. It was all carried out through the hole in the window by the rats.

Another time I had killed an opossum and had thrown it out in the ditch behind the house. We had an egg man by the name of Porter, who came there and saw the dead opossum. "How much for that animal?"

"Oh, give me a quarter," I said.

He took it, and the next time he came back he said, "That was delicious, do you have any more?"

One time I lost my billfold with $7.00 in it. That was a disaster. I found it two years later, but could not get the bills redeemed because they were all rotted. At that time the church had a collector to go around to Amish homes to collect alms money. We were assessed according to our financial worth. My share was at one time ten cents. The collector was Doddy Eli, or Eli Miller, who was Emma Miller's dad, and sometimes I did not have a dime. But things did improve some because of the good crops.

In 1943 we left the Amish Church and joined the Canaan Beachy Church. When the Amish preacher came to us, wanting to know what the problem was, I simply said, "We want a car." We bought a 1936 Chevy, but to us it was like a Cadillac. Later we bought a 1942 Ford.

At that time I was not a born-again Christian, but I think Martha was. In the Beachy Church we had services every Sunday morning and services on Sunday evenings, and we had Sunday school. But the services were still in German. My parents were very upset that we left the Amish. I don't want to say too much, but they almost disowned us. We regret those things and I feel now that we could have helped matters, if we would have had a different attitude. Again, I say I regret some of the attitudes we had. Martha's parents were different. Oh, yes, they would have preferred for us to stay with the Amish, but they accepted it more lovingly.

Soon after we joined the Beachy Church, I became a born-again Christian. Martha and I made some goals and prayers about our life together. One was to work together in regards to buying any major item, always to agree before we made a major purchase, and to agree on things in the presence of our children. One of my goals and prayers was that we could become financially stable, so as to be prepared in case of my death. Knowing I was a bleeder, Martha could become a young widow. And most of all, that our children would grow up and walk in the truth. John says, "I have no greater joy than to see my children walking in the truth."

But then there was a problem. Dad said we could not stay on his farm. Dad sold the farm to Fred Overholt. So by the end of 1943 we had to move. After we had left the Amish Church and joined the Beachy Church, Emory Yutzy lent us money to buy a tractor and other things. So we left that farm with many fond memories, and were able to stock up pretty well with borrowed money from Emory Yutzy. Emory and Robert Kaufman were the ministers at the Beachy Church.

In 1944 Edna was born. I had gone to an auction in the afternoon, and while I was gone Martha went into labor. She asked the neighbor to go get my Mom, Lizzie Helmuth, and called Dr. Karrer. By the time I came home, we had another daughter. It was a toss-up whether we'd name her Emma or Edna, so we pulled papers to decide, and it turned out Edna. I suppose that's the reason Edna likes to go to auctions today.

One day that winter, I was driving to Plain City. As I went around a curve in front of the Baptist Church on Plain City-Georgesville Rd., the car slid on ice, and I hit a tree. I had bruises and bumps, and suffered from internal bleeding. I was in the hospital for a week.

The next spring, we moved to the farm on Lucas Rd., owned by George Stoker, where the Joe Detweiler family later lived. It was all grain farming, no livestock. I had bought a new John Deere tractor and plow and cultivator after we joined the Beachy Church, for $825. I bought an Allis Chalmbers combine for $450, and did quite a lot of custom work. It was during the war, and machinery was almost impossible to buy because they were making war machinery. You had to put your name in at the dealer and wait your turn. But we were on a trip to Michigan and passed a dealer that had a combine. I bought one, and that was the way I got my combine.

From then on, some people went to Michigan and bought combines and balers. Even at farm auctions, there was a price ceiling on machinery. The auctioneers had books showing what they should sell for. They would announce the ceiling price. Lots of hands went up. You put your name on a slip of paper and handed it in. They put the papers in a container and drew out one. That was the winning buyer. At first the auctioneer would say, "We are selling you the plow and giving you the tractor," but the government stopped that quick.

Many times drivers would take a load of Amish people to the auction to put their names in. One time my brother Ben had two loads of people go to a sale near Washington Courthouse. I think there must have been 2000 people there. They announced the price on a Massey Harris tractor and we all put our names in a milk can. They shook the can and drew out a paper. "Ben Helmuth, Plain City, Ohio." Ben was the winner and drove that tractor home about 60 miles. He used it many years.

I also bought a corn picker in Michigan. I did a lot of custom corn-picking and combining for other people. At this time we did have electricity and phone service, but no indoor bathroom. Gasoline was rationed. They would allot so much to farmers, according to the amount of acres each had.

We lived on the Stoker farm for two years. We were in a little better condition financially, but my parents still were very much opposed to our church life. Especially my sister Emma would make far-out statements about us. We had to put up with lots of bad feelings toward us.

Jakie started school and could not speak English. One morning the alarm clock rang. It's time to get up. Short night, I thought, but up we got. I walked way back to the pasture for the cows. They were stubborn, but I got them in the stall. Martha said, "My cow is not giving much milk." Mine were not either. We put the milk in the tank, but there was not as much as usual. But we had milk ready for the milkman. We went back to the house and the clock showed 2 a.m. The children had played with the clock. So we went back to bed.

3

Young Ambitions

Our Move to Buchanan County, Iowa

In the winter of 1945/46, many of the Amish in Ohio were moving to Buchanan Co., Iowa. One of my sisters, the Freeman Detweilers, went. My Dad said if we would come back to the Amish and move to Iowa, he would buy a farm, and we could move on it and farm 50/50. That sounded so good that we decided to make the move. So in the fall of '45 we sold out and went back to the Amish. In November we had an auction. We sold all of the machinery, hay, corn, and grain. In the meantime I had bought a new Allis-Chalmers tractor. The tractor and picker had price ceilings on them, and were raffled off. Eli N. Yutzy drew the tractor ticket, but who got the picker I don't remember.

A semi-truck from Iowa came in to haul our furniture, miscellaneous items, and horse and buggy. The cost was $175. In November I went to Iowa on the train, to attend the auction at the farm that my Dad had bought. I got on the train at Plain City and went to Oelwein, and Freeman Detweiler, my brother-in-law, picked me up. He took me home and then, the next day to the auction. Phil Van de Vord was the man's name who had owned the farm. I bought some things, and the Fairbanks State Bank did the clerking, as was customary then. I did not have to pay cash, but just gave a note to pay later.

Back in Plain City, Martha was getting things ready to move. I think we moved to Iowa in February of 1946. The family went by train. About six other families from Plain City also went. When we got there, lots of people had gathered to unload the truck. It was below zero and was real winter weather.

The weather was cold, but the people's hearts and hospitality were warm. We really felt welcome. We had company about every evening, and the change of climate made me very sleepy; sometimes I could hardly make it. I went to auctions about every day to buy horses and machinery.

We were a young couple with five children. The house was a nice little house, but still with no indoor toilet or running water. We did have an icebox and just a very simple line of furniture. We had a basement and two bedrooms downstairs. Jakie and Willie slept upstairs, but the upstairs was not furnished out. We had a washhouse and walkway to the outhouse. The soil was rich, and Martha always had a very nice garden. We had a windmill right outside the house, which pumped the water to a large water trough out by the barn. We had a very nice hog house. The barn had six or seven horse stalls, about ten cow stations, and a loaf shed.

The water pipes had to be four feet underground to keep them from freezing in the winter. We also had to have a heater in the water trough to keep the water from freezing. Farming was very different; the soil had some sand in it, which made it easy to till. There were no thistles and we used no fertilizer.

The church rules were different. No storm fronts in buggies, no 'zibbel-kabb' (stocking caps); no generators were allowed, and no bicycles. No hiring of combines, corn pickers or hay balers. No tractors were to be used for belt power, but they allowed large motors mounted on wheels that were moved around with horses. The balls on the harness hames had to be removed. No cigarettes were allowed, but chewing tobacco, pipes, and cigars were allowed. The men had to wear big black hats, and the women wore bonnets and shawls. Church, too, was held every two weeks, and there was no Sunday school. On alternate Sundays, people would go visiting. There were no invitations; you started out, and if someone was not at home, then on to the next place. It was always for a meal. We had lots of company.

Now to the farming. The farm had 80 acres with lots of stones. There was one stone in the community that you could turn a 4-horse team around on.

When plowing, one tug on one side of the horses was tied to the double tree with a wire, so when you hit a stone, the wire would break, acting as a break-away link. We sowed oats with an end-gate seeder on back of the wagon, spreading the oats on the soil, then discing the oats into the ground.

We had good crops. Grain was cut with a binder and threshed. Corn was husked by hand. Martha helped me. I told her one time, "If you help me real good, come Christmas you will be surprised." And she was. I bought her nothing. She did forgive me. I have made it up since then. Those were interesting days.

With winter coming on we always prepared for cold weather. Days were spent shoveling snow, taking care of the livestock, and going to auctions. Every Wednesday was auction day in Oelwein, and I'd never miss. I'd buy colts, calves and other things to make a few dollars. We had a beautiful sorrel team that would make any Amishman proud. They were registered, but I could not keep the papers on them; that was against church rules. We would go to Oelwein to do shopping and would stop on the way home at Dairy Queen; boy, that was a treat. Ten cents a cone.

Some of our best friends were Joe C. Yoders and Amos Bontragers. A year after we moved to Iowa, our very good friends, Monroe & Lizziann Kurtz, moved out with their family. Their truck was delayed, so they stayed at our house a few days. One blizzard-like winter day Monroe and I decided to go to an auction 14 miles away. I drove, and Monroe held the buggy robe as a storm front on the buggy. Monroe had icicles on his beard. We got to the sale, but it was called off because of the weather. Long trip, no sale, and two Amish guys almost frozen.

There was a real snowstorm in 1947. It snowed and blew and drifted up to 10-foot drifts, and about 3 feet on the level. Trains were derailed, and delivery trucks were stranded. The drivers stayed in some of the Amish homes. After the first snow, the sun melted it on top. Then it froze and snowed again. It did that three times. It was just like a large chunk of ice. The milk truck drove on top of these huge drifts.

Our house was heated with a coal stove. We all slept around the stove. All we could do was keep warm and take care of the livestock. One night about 2 a.m., we heard motors down the road. I got up to see how they would open the road. They had a huge plow which backed up, rammed into a drift, and big ice chunks flew. They kept that up all through the night. Before the roads were opened, our neighbor Levi Yoder needed a doctor for the birth of a child. They cut the fence and took two horses in a sled and brought the doctor to their house. I think the cost of the delivery was about $25.

The snowstorm lasted about a week. After the snow melted, the roads were very muddy, as they were not paved. Some of the roads were so muddy that we would get stuck with a horse and buggy.

I had rented a pasture field from Adam Bontrager for the coming summer. I went to sales to buy horses, colts and calves, putting them in the pasture for the summer, and then selling one at a time and making a little money. I would advertise to buy buggy robes and would get letters telling me what they had and the price they wanted. I sent them a check and would receive the robes by return mail. At times, I would have a dozen or more robes upstairs. Then I sold them for a little profit. With my buying and selling, along with the farming, raising hogs, milking, and having chickens, we started to gain a little financially.

In the fall of 1947, 40 acres across the road came up for sale. I wanted that badly, but didn't have enough money. I went to Gideon Yutzy and told him about it. He said, "How much do you need?" The price was $112.50 per acre, which would make it $4500. He went to the house and got me a check for $4500, and I signed a note and went home. I asked him how much the interest would be. "I won't charge you interest, since you're a young man just starting out," he told me. That was my first land purchase.

A year later, in 1948, we bought the farm from Dad, so then we owned 120 acres. As a young couple with 5 children, we felt we had the cat by the tail. With hard work and a helping wife and 5 children, we were gaining financially.

One day as I was working in the field next to Joe Yoder's field, Joe and I let the horses rest, and we visited, and Joe said, "Why don't you go with me after harvest to Colorado?" After discussing it with Martha, I decided to do that. So after harvest, Joe and I took the train and went to Hutchinson, Kansas. There,

Chris Yoder, Joe's brother, joined us, and we went to Manitou Springs, Colorado. We got a cabin and cooked our meals and did sight-seeing. We made an arrangement with a Greyhound Line Van to go to Cripple Creek and Canon City. Four others from Cleveland, Ohio were with us. We went over Sky Line Drive. It was on a high mountain ledge and the driver sped along fast. He told us that a car went over the edge once, and they never saw it again, and he was joking about the drive. I started to get sick, vomited, and was not enjoying it one bit.

We got to Canon City. They took me to the drugstore and got me some Alka-Selzer. I was beginning to get homesick. We got back to our cabin, and I did not enjoy myself after that. It was time to start home.

Joe said we would go to Kansas and stay over Sunday, then home to Iowa on Monday. I said, "You can stay in Kansas as long as you like, but I'm going home." We went to the bus station. I got on a bus and got to Hazelton, Iowa on Sunday at 2 a.m. I hired a cab to take me home. When I walked in the door, Martha was standing inside. We fell into each other's arms and cried. "Martha, I promise I will never go without you again, as long as I live."

In the spring the roads were very muddy. When going to church in the spring, we had to wear four-buckle overshoes. The north-south road was called Hook and Eye Road, now known as Amish Boulevard. Lester Detweiler had the harness shop, where I got my harness work done. Emanuel Miller had the buggy shop, and he did my buggy. A man by the name of Mr. Peters had a grocery truck, coming to the house with a good line of groceries. The basement was well-stocked with canned goods, so we were always prepared when company came. Sometimes we would have 4 or 5 couples come unexpectedly.

One day, we as a family all went to Littleton on a picnic and fishing trip. On the way home as we passed two friends' houses, we yelled for them to come over and eat fish. But we did not have any fish. They came. No fish, but good fellowship.

Jakie, Willie, Carolie, and Betty went to school in a schoolhouse just a fourth mile up the road. That school was more like a playhouse than a school. The teacher would let the children go to the barn next door and play, while she slept. One day, Martha found the boys' undershorts under the mattress. The boys said the children in school teased them, saying they were wearing bloomers. I guess wearing underwear was something new to those children.

MARTHA:

We lost three babies in the four years we lived in Iowa. In 1946, we had a baby girl. She was a Downs Syndrome baby, born at home. We had a woman doctor. In 1947, another baby girl was born at the Oelwein Hospital. It was a hard birth, and it took me quite a while to get my strength back. Then in 1949 we had a stillborn son. During the last months of the pregnancy I was filling up with fluid. If I wanted to go to the doctor, I had to put my shoes on as soon as I got out of bed, or I couldn't get them on. My legs were stretched way out of proportion. Once the baby was born, I started passing fluid. I think I lost 17 pounds the first few days. I carried each baby to about 8 months.

The doctor then suggested we take tests, and we found out I was Rh negative, and Eli was Rh positive. Either I would poison the child, or the child poisoned me.

We also had Scarlet Fever while we lived in Iowa. We were quarantined several weeks. I think the children all had it, except for Betty.

4

Amish Man Wants Job

Move Back to Plain City, Ohio

In the spring of 1949, I was beginning to get dissatisfied and started thinking about moving back to Plain City, Ohio. We decided to sell the farm. During the summer, Joni Miller drove in and asked about it. I told him I wanted $225 per acre, which was $27,000. He said he hated to buy it if we were moving away. I told him that we were moving anyway, and someone would buy it. He sat there on the buggy and then said he would take it. Today the farm is owned by Adin Helmuth, my nephew.

Knowing we would have an auction, I hired someone with a pick-up baler to bale the hay, although that was against the rules of the church. I had to make a confession. I regret that I went against the church rules, but I know the Lord has forgiven me.

We had a large auction. We sold all our possessions but the furniture and sold 3 or 4 wagons' full of collars, harnesses, and many horse-related items. Also, we sold horses, colts, cows, calves, hogs, chickens, and all the implements, grain, and the baled hay. I had a beautiful sorrel team of horses that was hard to see go. We had a large crowd and things sold high. Oh yes, we sold the buggy and about 15 or 20 buggy robes that I had bought earlier.

We hired a trucker to haul our furniture to Plain City. We left Iowa with mixed feelings and many friends, and many fond memories. I think it was in

December of 1949. The family went by train. At that time Plain City had a depot, where you could get off the train.

As I was writing this about Iowa, I was reminded over and over how the Lord blessed us. How the children stood with us, and how some of the Amish helped us financially. It was in Iowa that we got on our feet financially.

In Plain City we bought the Dave Garver place on Rosedale-Plain City Road, where Rex Toops now lives. We paid $8,500 for the 30 acres.

After we moved to Plain City, we attended the Amish Church only about six months. Then we joined the Canaan Beachy Church and had a gasoline-powered washing machine. One morning I had trouble getting it started. In disgust, I told Martha that if we had to have a washer like that to be a Christian, then it's hard to be a Christian. I called the electric company about getting electricity. They said we needed to get an easement from Alvin Kramer for a line of about a fourth mile, up to Amish Pike, and it would cost $450. I went to Alvin, and he said he would give an easement. That was terrific. We had the house wired and had electricity in a short time. We also got a phone, the old wooden box crank type, with 8 or 9 on the line. When the phone rang, you could hear others also pick up the receiver. It had the right name, "Party Line."

We did a lot of work on the house. We put new siding on, put in built-in cabinets and added a bathroom. For the first time in our 14 years of marriage, we had a bathroom and cabinets. We put up a new 3-car garage. I bought a new Ford tractor, and a new Nash car. It was black and looked like a bathtub upside down on wheels.

Jakie and Willie did the farming after school. All five children, Jake, Willie, Carolyn, Betty and Edna, went to Oak Grove School, a small country school, where Mary Yutzy was the teacher. She was a super teacher, different from the Iowa teacher. The school was about one mile from our house. It is still there, across from the Noah Troyer farm.

MARTHA:

In November of 1950, our daughter Martha was born. The doctor knew we had the Rh problem, so he periodically took blood tests and all showed clear. Martha was born at Grant Hospital, and they checked her blood right after she was born. They rushed her to Children's Hospital where they exchanged all her blood. The doctor told us not to rejoice yet, but to wait for about a week. Well, she came through it, and it was some exciting day when we brought her home! I remember the first time she cried. We were at the table eating, and everyone ran to see how she looked when she was crying. They had to take her back and give her another transfusion. She had a lot of colds. We didn't take her away much that winter. I had never thought we'd have a live baby again. We praise and glorify God for her.

In the spring of 1950 they started building the Ranco plant in Plain City. On a Friday I went out where they had started to build. I walked in, a bit nervous, because I had never worked at a place like that. I asked for a job. The guy said, "Grab your shovel and go to work." He was a big man with a gruff voice, and it scared me. I told him I could not stay then, as I had to go home and tell my wife. He said to come back Monday. I went back Monday, and went to work. He was a slave driver. I was not afraid of work, because I was used to hard work, but I was not used to the rough language. He soon saw that I was not afraid of work, and he treated me well. He wanted me to bring a can of water each day, as they did not yet have water. Every few days he would hand me a $20 bill. I worked there all year, and helped build all those buildings, now known as Ranco, Inc.

In the summer of 1951 we joined the United Bethel Mennonite Church. We left the Beachy Church with a good church letter, and to this day we have many fond memories of the Beachy Church. That summer Myron Augsburger held tent meetings on the old Jake Farmwald land. At those meetings I re-dedicated my life to the Lord, and had a very good experience with the Lord. This was a change in my life. I think the same year we had revival meetings at United Bethel with Howard Hammer as the evangelist, and Bill (Willie) accepted Christ, at the age of 11. He had a real experience.

By then the Ranco building was finished, and I went inside to work. My number was 30010. I still have my badge and number somewhere. I still had a beard. I remember one day when I came to work, Freida Beachy said, "Eli, you might as well cut it all off instead of a little at a time."

I went home and cut it off. I think my daughter Martha was glad, because when I held her, I would rub my beard against her face. She would say, "No, no, it itches!"

Jake was 13 and Bill was 12. They did the farming on our little farm and were going to school. We had church and Sunday school every Sunday at United Bethel. Andrew Farmwald and Enos Yoder were the ministers. I think at this time I was working night shift at Ranco, which was not the best, because the children went to school in the morning before I got up, and I went to work in the afternoon before they came home. Martha did a good job of managing things. Every year I got two weeks' of paid vacation time. We took several trips to New York where Martha has a sister, Mary Mast. I remember one time when the family came to Ranco at midnight to meet me, and we drove to Buffalo, New York and got there at 8:00 in the morning.

I had several severe injuries and bleeding problems while working at Ranco. One time a barrel of metal dropped on my foot. I was in the hospital with lots of bleeding. That was before Factor 9 was manufactured, and sometimes there was no blood in the blood bank. They had a lot of trouble getting my bleeding stopped. My Ranco insurance always paid the bills. Even our baby births were paid by them, and all our doctor bills.

MARTHA:

In October of 1952 Bonnie was born. My blood tests showed I had antibodies, so we knew she had to have her blood exhanged right after she was born. She was born at Grant Hospital, and they took her to Children's to have her blood exchanged. I had a navel hernia, and I had surgery to have it repaired, and was put on another floor after surgery. Eli was waiting until I would be brought into my room, and looked in several times, but couldn't see me, as I was lying close to the wall. I was wondering, "Where is Eli?"

Finally, Eli went to the nurses and asked where his wife was. They said, "Oh, is that your wife? We thought you were a priest." Eli had his straight-cut coat on. I don't know how long it was before we got together, but it was a long time, we thought. The children had the measles when we brought Bonnie home, so they had to stay upstairs a few days. Dr. Karrer always called Bonnie and Martha his miracle babies. And we did, too.

In 1953 we sold the 30-acre farm, which we called the Garver farm, to Andrew Yutzy. We bought a farm of approximately 100 acres, over close to the town of Watkins. I think we paid $17,000 for it, but it was very run-down.

Weeds were as high as some buildings. There was no bathroom, but we put one in. I remember going to First National Bank in Marysville, asking to borrow money to put a bathroom in. Homer Viers said he had never seen me before. I said if I get this money, he probably wouldn't ever see me again. He shoved a note out to me, said to sign it, and I got the money and went home and built a new bathroom. We also put new cabinets in, and built a 4-car garage. We bought a John Deere tractor, and the boys farmed the land.

I continued to work at Ranco and had a good paying job. I was advanced to press set-up man. I also worked at various jobs in the area. I did some hauling of the Amish, and hauled Chris Gingerich quite a bit. On one occasion I took Chris to Columbus where he bought an old car to be used as a power unit. I took my brother Al along to drive it home. On the way home Al failed to stop for a school bus and got a ticket.

When I would take Chris on short trips, he wanted Martha and Bonnie to go along. They could sing so well, and he always enjoyed their singing. I took Chris to London, a neighboring town, one day, and I told him that I had to be back at 2:00 because of working at Ranco at 3:00. He did not show up at the car, so I went home without him. He told me later he got a ride home with someone else. He held nothing against me.

In 1954 Jake became 16 years old. Now we had a boy with the young folks! Jake was a real mama to Martha and Bonnie. From now on I will refer to my wife as Mom, because one of our daughters is Martha. The five older children did a good job of taking care of the two 'little ones', as we called them. So Mom and I could go away alone sometimes. The children went to the Watkins School about one mile up the road.

In November of 1954, for our vacation we decided to take a trip to Florida. We wanted to see what it looked like. We took Betty, Edna, Martha and Bonnie with us, and Jake, Bill, and Carolyn took care of the farm. We had a Dodge pick-up truck at home, so the children had a way to get around and go to church. We left for Florida, which they called 'The Land of Sunshine'. We got to Pinecraft in Sarasota and stayed in a shack on Bimini Street. The house was on stilts, had a pot-bellied stove, and it was a cold, damp winter. I mean winter. It was so cold and damp, you could almost wring water out of the clothes.

There was no sunshine; it was just bitter cold.

After a few days, we decided we did not have to stay there. We left the children with a neighbor and went south. We got to Key West and it was no better, as they had no covers on the beds. After suffering from the bitter cold, we decided to fly to Cuba. The plane was a 2-motor prop plane, and it shook and rattled like a manure spreader. We got to Havana, Cuba, and guess what? It was just as cold, and we had no windows in the motel, just bars. We got someone to drive us around the island and spent two days there. We flew back to Key West, got the car, drove to Sarasota, picked up the children, and took off for home and a warm house. That night we slept warm and said they can give Florida back to the Indians. It was so good to be home, united with our family again. Henry Yoder had told me they had given a nickel an acre when they bought Florida, and I decided they got taken.

At Christmas that year I bought Mom a new Singer sewing machine, which I remember very well was $309, a high price for us.

I thank the Lord for a very close-knit family. Here on the Watkins farm we did no livestock farming; had only one cow for milk. Jake did not like to drive our Nash car; he said the young people made fun of it. So I bought Jake a 1951 Ford. He was working for Bill Limes, a plumber.

One winter evening Mom and I, with Edna, went to an auction in the neighboring town of Delaware. Jake had gone to the young people's meeting at church, and the rest of the children had stayed home. We got home about midnight and saw furniture and clothes piled up out in the garage. "What's wrong?" A fire had broken out in the house.

The two little ones, Martha and Bonnie, usually slept downstairs, but Carolyn and Betty had taken them upstairs that night with them. Carolyn and Betty were upstairs as well. In the middle of the night, they were awakened by smoke. Bill was a hero; he got them all to run downstairs, but he could not get to the phone because of the smoke. He guided them out through the smoke, to safety. He warned the girls to keep the doors and windows closed, so as not to give the fire a draft. He ran barefoot to the neighbors to call the Fire Department.

Later, Bill said that if Martha and Bonnie had slept downstairs, they probably would have suffocated. He told me how fast he had run to the neighbors, barefoot. I said, "Did you pass any cars?"

We had to replace the cabinets and some walls, but the family was safe. Praise the Lord. I feel the Lord has given Jake and Bill a gift of caring, as they always loved to take care of their little sisters.

In the summer of '55 we, along with the five girls, took a trip to Colorado. The boys again stayed home to do the farming. We went to Kansas and stopped at Mom's relatives, and then on to Manitou Springs to spend about ten days there. We rented a cabin and took a tour of Seven-Falls and Pikes Peak, the Royal Gorge and the Garden of the Gods. The girls liked to go to the park and watch the Indians dance in the evenings. We had a good two-week vacation with pay.

In 1956, for my vacation, Mom and I took Chris and Clara Gingerich to Portland, Maine, to visit their son Bill, who was in I-W Service. The children stayed home to do the farming. I think back how wonderful that was that the children did that and we could go away. That was a different experience for us, driving through New York City, along the coast up to Maine.

At one place we stopped and went out deep-sea fishing. We had four or five ladies on the boat with us. Chris got sea-sick and started throwing up. He was lying in the boat, and even the ladies got soiled with vomit. Barely being able to say it, he said, "I'm, I'm so, so sick, I can't even pray."

When we got to Bill's place, he was glad to see us. He was homesick, and the other fellows were not very nice, and he felt out of place. We did have a good time and made friends with a couple named Carl and Grace Stonesifer. We kept contact with them for many years. We treasured that trip very highly. Back to Plain City, thanking the Lord for the safety.

My having had so many injuries at Ranco and bleeding experiences, the Industrial Commissioners started to complain. So, in August of 1956, they said I would have to go over to another department, sitting on a chair and assembling parts. That was not for me, but I said I would try it.

I was in Department 319 with all women. Their language was not very edifying, and I decided that wasn't for me. I went to the office and told them. They said I would be making a mistake if I quit, because I had high seniority.

But I decided to quit. I went home and told Mom that the world had caved in on me. She said she was glad I quit, because it was a dangerous job. That was September 6, 1956, after exactly 6 years of being inside.

I put an ad in the Columbus Dispatch: 'Amish Man Wants Job'. The very next day Bill Mueller called, "Come down, I want to talk to you." I went down to 2530 Fishinger Dr. in Columbus. Bill said, "I'll give you $3.00 per hour." I went to work for him the next day. My job was to drive truck, hauling lumber, and checking jobs; he was a house builder. I started to work September 8 or 9. I hauled lumber from Springfield, Ohio to the Columbus job sites. Later I also started doing ceramic tile work in bathrooms. At Thanksgiving he gave me a turkey, and at Christmas he gave me $500. The following year he gave me a brand-new truck for Christmas.

Bill was now 16, and we bought him a turquoise and white, 1958, hard-top Ford. A beautiful car. Bill really babied that car. Jake and Bill both had worked for the neighbors part-time. The girls kept saying Bill did nothing but torment them, get him out of the house. So one day Mom and I went to an auction, where they sold all kinds of tools, toys and games. We bought a big Erector set for Bill, and he got out of the girls' hair and spent night after night putting things together with his Erector set. He even made a baler that worked. I think that is when Bill first recognized his mechanical ability.

In the fall of '57, Dan Troyer, Abe Farmwald and Chauncey Headings came to us and wanted to sell us the two acres next to Andy Farmwald. They had been appointed to help Andy with his financial problems, so we bought those two acres for $2000.

That winter Mom and I took another trip to Florida, but we took no chances and stayed at a Howard Johnson motel. That was a beautiful winter; we really enjoyed that trip. Then in the summer of '58, we went to Colorado again for about two weeks.

We got a permit to build a house on the two acres and got Bill Mueller to build a house for us. We sold the farm on Watkins-New California Road and bought a house at 309 W. Main St. in Plain City. We lived there until the new house was finished. It was being built in the summer of 1959 and we moved to the new house in the fall. We rented the house in Plain City to someone else.

The new house had 3 baths, 4 bedrooms, with a 2-car garage. It was a ranch style house, costing $16,000.

About that time Carolyn started working for the Muellers at their house, and Mom and the girls started cleaning the houses he built. Jake attended Berlin Bible School in Berlin, Ohio. That fall Jake went to Meridian, Mississippi in Voluntary Service. Even though we wanted him to go into service, we really missed him.

The winter of 1959, Levi and Sarah Gingerich and we went to Montezuma, Georgia and to Bluntstown and Sarasota in Florida. We stayed in Hill-Top Kate's house. It was a very nice winter. We were gone about two weeks.

ELI AND MARTHA HELMUTH

THE HOME ON SMITH-CALHOUN RD.,
WHERE I GREW UP AS AN AMISH BOY.

THIS IS THE EARLIEST PICTURE I HAVE OF MYSELF, AT AGE 12.
I AM IN THE BACK ROW, FOURTH FROM THE RIGHT.

OUR FARMHOUSE IN BUCHANAN COUNTY, IOWA.
IT HAS BEEN REMODELED SINCE WE LIVED THERE.
(PHOTO −2001)

THE SCHOOLHOUSE JAKIE, WILLIE, CAROLYN,
AND BETTY ATTENDED IN IOWA.
(PHOTO −2001)

THE GARVER PLACE IN PLAIN CITY, OHIO,
WHERE WE LIVED FROM 1950-1952.

OUR CHILDREN IN 1951:
CAROLYN, JAKE HOLDING MARTHA, EDNA, BILL, BETTY.

OAK GROVE SCHOOL
WHERE OUR CHILDREN ATTENDED
WHILE WE LIVED AT THE GARVER PLACE.

WE ENJOYED MANY FAMILY OUTINGS.
HERE WE ARE HAVING A PICNIC AFTER A BOAT RIDE.

VISITING WITH MY BROTHER JONAS
IN BUCHANAN COUNTY, IOWA, AROUND 1950.

HERE I AM WITH MY PRETTY GIRL, IN THE 1950S.

OUR FAMILY IN THE 1950S
BETTY, ME HOLDING MARTHA,
MOM HOLDING BONNIE, EDNA, BILL.

OUR FARM ON WATKINS, NEW-CALIFORNIA RD.
WE LIVED HERE FROM 1953-1957.

THE HOME PLACE ON LAFAYETTE-PLAIN CITY RD.,
BUILT BY BILL MUELLER IN 1959.

HERE I AM IN FRONT OF PLAIN CITY AUCTION,
ON MAIN STREET IN PLAIN CITY, OHIO.

INSIDE PLAIN CITY AUCTION ON A SALE NIGHT,
WITH ANDY FARMWALD AS AUCTIONEER.

One of our favorite ways to relax –playing Scrabble.

Helping a Papua New Guinean woman at a 'mumu'.

ON ONE OF OUR MANY
TRIPS TO HAITI.

WHAT A VIEW FROM THE TOP!

THE WORDS SAY IT ALL . . .
WELCOME HOME, CHILDREN.

OUR
FLORIDA
HOME

OUR
OHIO
HOME

AT A FAMILY REUNION IN 1990, LEFT TO RIGHT: EDNA, BETTY, MOM, BILL, BONNIE, ME, JAKE, CAROLYN, MARTHA.

OUR FAMILY AT OUR 60TH ANNIVERSARY, LEFT TO RIGHT: CAROLYN, MOM, BONNIE, MARTHA, JAKE, BILL, ME, EDNA, BETTY.

FAMILY REUNION IN 1988.

MOM WITH CAROLYN, AND CLARA LOUISE YODER,
OUR ADOPTED DAUGHTER.

WE HAVE 18 GRANDCHILDREN AND 30 GREAT-GRANDCHILDREN.
HERE I AM WITH MY GRANDDAUGHTER RACHEL IN 1981.

WE HAVE LIVED A LONG AND INTERESTING LIFE.
GOD HAS BEEN VERY GOOD TO US AND BLESSED US IN MANY WAYS.

OUR CURRENT MODE OF TRANSPORTATION—
OUR TRUSTY THREE-WHEELERS.

5

Going, Going, Gone!

Plain City Auction

In the spring of 1960 Andy Farmwald would often come over on Sunday evenings and have coffee and talk. One evening we discussed about starting an auction. We decided to try it. So we rented a building from Walter Fee on Church St. in Plain City and advertised to have a sale on a Saturday afternoon. I was still working for Bill Mueller, but we did this auction work in the evenings. The first sale, I think we lacked about $50 each from making the expenses.

Our second auction we lacked about $30 each from making the expenses. The third sale we came out about even. We were paying $35 a month for the building. For the fourth sale, I had bought a dining room suite for $25 at a garage sale, and it brought $125 at the sale. Now that gave us courage. We were starting to make a little money. The auction was called Plain City Auction. We had one auction a month, the last Saturday of the month. Then Mr. Fee went up in rent. So we quit the auction but kept looking for another building.

Andy was in Illinois holding revival meetings when Johnny Michael got the Legion Hall on Maple St. for me. I called Andy and asked if I could have the sale myself and he be my auctioneer, and he said that was okay. So we started having sales at the Legion Hall once a month on Friday evenings. The young folks from United Bethel Mennonite Church served lunch.

Things started picking up. Even though I was working for Bill Mueller, in my spare time, I would go to garage sales and other sales to buy things. I also started getting more consignments. I would spend lots of evenings and Saturdays buying and getting things ready for the next sale. Things were getting better and better. We were not making much money, but I had a good job with Mueller, and Mom and the family stood by me and encouraged me.

Other happenings in the 60s: Jake got married to Lydiann Miller, a girl he met while in Meridian, Miss. Bill got married to Fanny Yutzy, a local girl. Carolyn went to El Dorado, Arkansas for Voluntary Service. Betty was at Eastern Mennonite College, Edna at Rockingham Memorial Hospital School of Nursing, both in Harrisonburg, Virginia. So Mom and I and the two little ones, Martha and Bonnie, were alone in that big house.

In 1963, we went to Virginia to visit Betty and Edna. As I was walking on North Main St. in Harrisonburg, I came past an antique shop, which had a 'For Sale' sign in the window. I stopped in, looked it over, and saw it was piled full of antiques and furniture. A lady by the name of Fannie Stickler was the owner. She said she wanted $8,000. That would be a big undertaking for us.

We went home and prayed about it. Then we went to the bank in Marysville and asked Homer Viers, whom I had deals with before, to borrow the money. He said yes. After a few calls to Harrisonburg, we went back to Virginia and bought the contents of the shop and changed the locks. Henry Diener was going to EMC, and he was an auctioneer. Henry had about four sales right there at the store, and we hauled about four truckloads home to Plain City. Bill Mueller let me use his truck without charge, gas only. We had taken two grandfather clocks up to a dorm room at EMC, where Moe Gingerich, Freeman Miller, and Nelson Miller were staying. They were attending school at EMC at the time.

We kept track of all our expenses, including lodging, eats, and any other expenses. When we got all finished with it, we had the big grandfather clock for our profit. That clock is now in our house in Florida.

In the meantime, someone stole some of the marble-top furniture. We were sure we knew what the deal was, but we did not want to go to court. Many items had cracked, and some of the things that Henry sold were not paid for.

But Mom always says, "But that got us started in antiques." Up until then we hardly knew what an antique was. So, Jake, the clock that belongs to you in Florida, is rich in history and is valuable. We had a lot of fun and experience through that deal. And we learned a lot about Harrisonburg, VA.

Mom clerked at the auctions. The sales were getting bigger. We were starting to get estates to sell from attorneys and banks. We were still having sales at the Legion Hall.

One week Mom and I went to Pennsylvania where we went to a big auction house at Bareville. On the way home we talked about someday having a building like that one. When we got to Plain City, an Oliver dealer was moving out of the Brigg Mercer Building at 145 E. Main St. We turned on Shepper Ave. and went to Mrs. Mercer, who had been my teacher in school. She was the owner of the building. "Mrs. Mercer, could I rent that building for an auction?"

She said, "You have got it." Were we happy! She said the rent was $75 per month. Praise the Lord; He answered our prayer and wish.

The next few days we worked hard, cleaning that building. It had grease all over the place. Our son Bill built a big platform in the main room, and bleachers with about 300 seats. We were in business! About two years before, Bill Mueller had changed his house-building business some. He hired everything done by contract. So I was doing the ceramic tile and marble sill work by contract. That gave me more time with the auction business.

We started having two auctions a month, the second and last Fridays of the month, and by 1963 I quit with Mueller because the auction was taking so much time. Mom and I dedicated the auction to the Lord, with the promise to run the auction on Christian principles and honesty.

The auction grew way over our expectations. We started getting dealers in from three or four southern states, and consignments from Columbus, Dayton, Springfield, Cleveland, and many other places. We got mail from far away; some were sent to the "Amish Auction in Plain City, Ohio." At many sales we had 500 to 600 people attending. We had a strict policy of no buy-bidding and no buy-backs; if consigned in, it must be sold. No smoking in the building. The rules we had, we enforced. I could write a whole book on experiences, but will give only a few.

One day we got a call about selling the estate of a former judge. We took it, because it was loaded with all kinds of furniture and antiques. We hauled it out and sorted it. Drawers were full of coins, handguns, rings, etc. We agreed to broom-clean the rooms and put trash in a walk-in closet with other things he said was trash.

His apartment was really loaded, and it was consigned to us by his brother who was an attorney. We sold all the things, including a small rug that was in that closet with things he called trash. That small rug brought $325 at the auction. We sent him the records and a check. He called and said that we paid him for some things that were not his, including that small rug that he called trash. We told him it was all his, hidden in drawers and with that trash in the closet. He said, "Now I see why people told me to send the things to Plain City Auction."

Another time a man from Fifth Ave. in Columbus called and said that he was in a meeting with the attorney of an estate. He said he was administrator of another estate and wanted us to sell the estate. We did, and it was one of the best we ever sold, lots of Heisey glass, Haviland china, and lots of jewelry and small valuable things in drawers.

Later we got a call from a store owner who said he had four showcases and wondered if we could pick them up. When we unloaded them, secret drawers at the bottom flew open, with watches, rings, jewelry, etc. We sent him receipts and a check. He also called and said we had paid him for a lot of extra items, when he only had four showcases. We told him that it was all his, in the secret drawers. He said, "Thank you. I have been hearing good things about you people."

By the way, those showcases were bought at the sale by us and were used at the Plain City Auction, on the stage for displaying fine items, for many years.

At one auction a woman looking through some books discovered a diamond ring in an envelope hidden in a book. The woman gave it to us and the next day Mom and I had the ring appraised and put in a safe deposit box. I called the attorney handling the estate and asked if he wanted the ring sold at the next auction. The attorney said "No, do not sell the ring." He explained that the ring meant a lot to the children and they had been blaming each other for taking the ring. I gave the ring to the attorney, who then paid us for the appraisal expenses, plus a gift of appreciation from the family. I then gave a token gift to the lady who had found the ring in the envelope.

One year, just before our December sale, I got a phone call from a woman wanting to consign some items, including a picture she had. I wanted her to wait until the next auction as the December one was already full and had been advertised. The woman insisted, saying she needed money for her children's Christmas presents. So the next day I drove to her house to pick up her items. I put the picture on the auction and was surprised to see it go up to around $750. An antique dealer from Columbus was the high bidder. I decided to take the check personally to the woman at her house. When I gave it to her, she started to cry. Thinking maybe she was disappointed, I asked how much she had hoped to get for it. She couldn't talk for crying, but her young son spoke up, "You know, Mom, you had hoped to get $50. Now we can really have Christmas!"

We never did advertise wanting things to sell. The people did our advertising. We had a policy that we would not sell televisions. When we took an estate, we said no to TVs. "Ok," they would say. "We still want you to handle the estate. We will send what you do not want to another auction." When we picked up contents from a whole houseful, they'd say to give the food and clothes to someone. We would give the clothes to City Missions, and the food we would give to the needy and keep some for ourselves.

I could mention hundreds of deals like those above, but will leave it at that.

I will mention a few not so pleasant deals. At this time we were selling from 5 p.m. to 2 a.m., in two and three rings. We had some very high-priced marble-top furniture and other antiques all set up for the sale, when someone came in and said, "You have some stolen things on display." This was about one hour before sale time. I told them they needed to get someone with authority, as I had a contract to sell those things. They got the sheriff and he came in and they marked the things that were thought to be stolen. We told the audience that the things marked could not be sold, because they were thought to be stolen. The guy who had consigned those things was sitting back on the bleachers. He got up and left at that point. On Monday the sheriff's department picked the things up. Later we got a letter from them, thanking us for the cooperation.

Another time, we had hauled a large estate in to sell. After it was in the building a lady came in the building and saw it. She said, "That is my merchandise." It did not belong to the people who had consigned it.

We were called into court about it. It was a second marriage deal. I said that I would not release it without being paid to haul it in. The judge sided with us. The people drew up a contract to haul it out and put it in storage. But it could not be sold until they paid us $500 for the hauling.

It went into storage for about two years, until the courts decided on the situation. After the courts had decided, they called us to come and pick it up again. I said, "No, I had it out here and you took it back. The only way we will sell it is if you bring it back out." They said ok, because they wanted us to sell it. They hauled it back out. After two years it had increased in value. There were a lot of oriental items, and it was a terrific sale, attended by attorneys and court people. So we got our $500 plus the commission on selling it. The Lord blessed us again.

Mom and I made two or three buying trips to New York, Maine, Vermont, and other New England states, buying Victorian furniture and other antiques to sell at the auction. Each time we would buy a truckload.

I was buying gas refrigerators, some from as far away as Colorado Springs and Macon, Georgia. I would make about 3 or 4 trips a year to Pennsylvania, where the Amish would buy the refrigerators. Sometimes Mom went along. I would then go to auctions and to wholesale places to buy a load to bring back. I would buy clocks, furniture and any bargains I could find. Again, Mom would go with me many times, making it a vacation. Those were very interesting times. All these trips were made between our auctions.

The very first time we went to Fred & Dottie's Wholesale Store in Douglasville, Pennsylvania, we had the truck loaded with good things to take back home. Mom wrote a check but made a mistake on it, and they wouldn't accept it. Lo and behold, it had been the last check in the checkbook and it was now torn up. We didn't want to unload, so they said if Mom stayed there as security, they would let me leave the things on the truck while I went back to the motel, 30 miles away, to get more checks. To this day we all laugh about it, and Dottie now says she would trust us to take the whole store and pay later.

After the sale was all set up each time, we would go out and do public relations visits to our customers. Back in the 50s and 60s, garage sales were starting to be held. I would hit all the sales and would get real bargains. I would check ads and run them down. Most of the merchandise in our earlier auctions was merchandise we bought at garage sales and through ads. Most of our furniture and antiques in our Plain City and Florida homes come from garage sales. We had two or three pickers who chased garage sales and ads and brought the things to our auction. They made a good living.

Edna was married to Moses (Moe) Gingerich August of 1966 and moved to an apartment in Columbus.

In May of '67 we, with about 20 others, took a trip to the Middle East. William McGraff was the tour leader. The trip was for 21 days. We were scheduled to go to Europe and the Holy Lands. We drove to Pennsylvania and Ivan Martins took us to New York. We flew to Rome, Italy, took in the sights, then flew to Cairo, Egypt, and took camel rides at the pyramids and saw a lot of other sights. We stayed at the Nile Hilton Hotel.

People were out on the street marching, saying, "We want war!" It was getting real tense at that time. We were scheduled to go to Jerusalem next, but the State Department said no, it was not safe. So the tour company offered us a choice of going to Athens, Greece, and taking a ship to the seven ports along the Aegean Sea, or going to Athens and staying there until it lined up with our schedule to go to Europe. We decided on the ship excursion.

We flew to Athens and boarded a large ship, stopping at 7 ports on the way to Turkey. One stop was Ephesus, where I got a haircut for a quarter. While we were on the ship, we celebrated my birthday, June 6, and the same day it was announced the 6-Day War broke out in the Holy Lands. So we rejoiced that we did not go to Israel. We docked in Turkey and took in lots of sights and went to a large flea market, where we bought two Mary Gregory vases. We returned to Athens by ship.

Then we flew to Europe, and by bus we took in many interesting places, like the flower auction and the cheese factory in Holland. We went to Witmarsen, where Menno Simons lived, and went to the church there. We were at the Mauri Damn, a miniature village. We traveled by train on a cog railroad to the Jungfrau, a high mountain in the Alps. We were in Zurich, Switzerland, where Felix Manz, an early Anabaptist, was drowned because of his faith.

We went to Amsterdam and the Hague, then back to Greece, where we stayed at a hotel. I called home to the auction, as it was sale night. I heard Johnny Mitchell the auctioneer crying out the sale. I heard him say, "Tell them we are praying for them."

Switzerland was my favorite, the beautiful snow-capped mountains, cows on the hillside, all having large cowbells on. All the homes had flower boxes under the windows, full of beautiful flowers. Holland was a great place for dairying. The houses and homes were built together. It was a wonderful trip, but we were glad to be home again. Ivan Martins picked us up again in New York, and we drove home from there. We have many fond memories of that trip and the people who were on the trip with us.

The auctions back home had gone well. Robert Sweeney, whom I had trained, had run the auction. Several years ealier Bob had been watching a local policeman practice for a charity auction and thought he could do just as well. He started attending our auctions and one day came to me and asked if he could try auctioneering at one of our sales. I decided to give him a chance. I announced to the audience, "Here's a boy from Hilliard who says he wants to be an auctioneer. Let's see what he can do." He sold for about ten minutes and did well. Bob started working for me and stayed with me for the next 6 years.

By this time we had bought the auction building from Mrs. Mercer. At this time we always had our last sale of the year on the second Friday night of the month. So after the sale we would take the records with us and leave for Florida, doing the bookwork at the motel, and finishing in Florida. So that gave us four weeks until the sale in January.

Johnny Michael was a good friend and a real estate dealer. He came to me and said he had a bargain, and I should buy it. And I did buy it. A nice house at 224 South Chillicothe St. in Plain City, which was across the street from the city firehouse. I think we paid about $12,000 for it. We rented it out.

In the winter of '69 Mom and I went to Florida again. We stayed in a house on Graber St., owned by Clarence Weaver. Passing by a house with a 'For Sale' sign, we called the real estate lady and made an appointment to see it. We had no intention of buying a house when we went to Florida. We bought the house for $8,500, made a deposit, and told Clarence Weaver that we didn't need his house after a certain date. We waited for the closing day, but they put us off again and again. The agent said they had a snowstorm in Ohio, where the owner lived, and he could not get out to sign the papers. It went on and on. Finally she called and said the owner sold it, by-passing her. She wanted to go to court, but we said no. So the deal was off and she gave our deposit back.

We had to move out of where we were, so we went to a very small room which had only a bedroom and a toilet, so small you had to back in. Next, we moved to a small trailer, which is just one block north of where we now live on Beneva Road. Beneva Road was just a lane at that time.

Walking up the street one day, a man was putting a 'For Sale' sign on a house. I asked how much he wanted for the house, and he said it had a vacant lot behind it, that goes with the house, and he wanted $8,000 for the house and lot. I called Lester Miller, who lived in Plain City, and asked how much it would be to paint that house. He said $400. I went back and told the man I would give him $7,600. He said that was ok. That is the house Lester Wengerd now lives in, and the vacant lot is where our house is located. Aaron Kaufman handled the transaction for us, and we let him have the house to rent. We went back home to Ohio, not believing we had bought a house in Florida.

That first winter, Bob and Fannie Miller lived in our little house on Beneva Rd. Atlee Mullets put new cabinets in and I went to Haiti with some others to build a church. Mom stayed with Bob and Fannie. I got back from Haiti and spent time in Florida until it was time to head home for the January sale.

Happenings in the 70s: We bought a new GMC pick-up truck and purchased 20 acres of land, adjacent to our place in Plain City, with the idea of some day building an auction house. We bought it from Jonas Troyer and rented it to Sherman Schrock. After much persuasion and Mom promising me they could run the sale this one time without me, I went with Allen Yutzy, Leroy Mast, and Johnny Miller to Stirling Lake in Canada for ten days to do some volunteer work. We had lots of car trouble on the way, but we had a good time. Allen tipped the boat and we ended up in the water. We did have some very good experiences.

The next winter Ed Slabachs and we went to Costa Rica. Betty was there teaching school. It was a very different culture. Ox carts were used for hauling merchandise. We rented a car and went out to the Beachy Amish settlement. It was very interesting to visit with them. Little Amish children were playing in a sandbox and spoke 3 languages, Pennsylvania Dutch, Spanish, and English. We flew back to Miami, then went to Haiti. It was Mom's first trip to Haiti. A very poor and different country. Back home again. Praise the Lord for a good trip.

One evening a guy came to the auction and got a number with a false driver's license. Number 40 was his buyer's number. He bought a lot of things; we always handed the items to the people as they bought. After the sale #40 had not paid his bill, and the merchandise was gone. So the next day we called the sheriff and in two days they knew who it was. The sheriff picked him up plus the merchandise and took him to court.

We had to appear, along with the clerk and the auctioneer. He had a jury trial, and they found him guilty and the judge sentenced him to one year. We got the items back but that bothered me. I regret that I signed against him. I promised the Lord I would not do that again.

Later a guy from Kentucky gave me a bad check for $3,000. The judge said that if we came to Kentucky and signed a warrant, he would get the money for us. We decided against going. We lost the $3,000, but we had peace and the Lord blessed us.

In the winter of '73 Jerry Yoders, Grant Gingerichs and we went to Puerto Rico, sight-seeing. We had a good trip. Grant was a building contractor. We asked him if he could get a permit to build a house on our vacant lot in Florida. He said he could. So we drew up a plan and he gave us a price. He got a permit and we stayed a week longer to pick colors and other important things. So the next year, 1974, he built the house. He agreed to build the 2-bedroom/2-bath house for $14,000. Were we ever happy with it when we got there and saw our new house! Later in October we took a load of furniture down for the house.

Before the house was finished, we got a letter from the state of Florida, saying that they wanted 17 feet in front of the little house, because they were going to widen Beneva Road. We signed the offer and got a good price. That winter they were working on the road, and much noise was going on. They planted the three palm trees in front of the little house over to the north side of the church. They are still there.

In the summer of '74 we took a trip to Virginia Beach, Virginia, Delaware, and other eastern states. I also took my brother Ben and his wife to Virginia to visit some of their friends. That winter we went to Florida again. At that time we lived in the back part of the new house. Leroy and Sue Mullet lived in the front part all year. We just stayed about a month.

That summer I took some Amish folks to Jamesport, Missouri, and they bought some farms. A saying I had was, "The Amish custom is to work and slave to make all the money you can, 'til you have six months left on the rocking chairs. You rock for six months, then they bury you and run for the estate."

Mom and I decided that would not be our goal. When Bonnie, who is the youngest, got married or left home, we were going to sell out and enjoy our retirement. So when Bonnie got married to Ivan Yoder, we were only 56 years old! Now what? Mom said that was our goal and prayer, the Lord had blessed us, and we had worked hard. Let's do it.

"Oh my, Mom, we are too young."

"So what," she said, "Let's have a good retirement and do what our goal was." So we sold the auction business to Bob Sweeney, but kept the building and rented it to Bob. After the last sale, we took off for Florida. We had had the auction for 15 years.

6

Home Sweet Home

Our Traveling Years

That winter while we were in Florida, Wayne Kaufman called and asked if I would serve on the Son Light Mission Board. I accepted. I attended meetings two times a year, and was on the board for 12 years. I had many good experiences and made many trips to Haiti. That winter we bought two duplexes and four apartments in Florida on School Ave. We rented them out.

When we got home to Plain City that spring, we put a camper on the truck and took off for Alaska. We did have some mixed feelings, as the Alaska Highway was all dirt and gravel. No pavement. Marvin Troyer had made a large shield for the front of the truck to protect the windshield. The road was rough and the gas prices were high.

Our goal was to travel 100 miles a day. When we got to the Highway and saw the stones fly when someone passed us, we stopped and had a higher shield put on. Everyone that we met was very friendly as they had to go through the same problems. Even though we had tape around the windows and doors, every time we stopped, everything inside was very dusty.

We went all the way to Fairbanks, and there we got a plane to go to the North Slope, which was an Eskimo village with oil fields. Back to Fairbanks, then to Anchorage, where we went to an auction. From there we went to Homer, down the spit, they called it, about 100 miles, a big fishing port. Dan and Elsie Gingerich lived there at the time. They invited us for supper, and that was a real treat, so far away from home.

At White Horse we put the camper on the train, went through the valleys and former gold fields to Skagway, where we put the camper on a large boat, with maybe 200 or so other vehicles. It took two days and two nights to get back to the mainland.

We sold the truck and camper to Moe and Edna who were then living in Bailey, Colorado. We stayed a week or two and then from there we took the bus home. We had been gone about three months.

We left that fall again for Florida where we celebrated our 40th wedding anniversary. Before we left I had written a poem. I gave it to Mom one night at a motel. She had to cry. I guess you would call that our 40th honeymoon, but the 39 honeymoons before that were probably spent under a full moon shocking wheat, cutting corn, and other hard work.

A Truly Good Wife

I have found a truly good wife;
She is worth more than precious gems.
Her husband does trust her;
She does satisfy her husband's every need.
She never hinders him, but always stands
by him to raise seven children.
She buys yardgoods and makes clothes for all the family.

She rises before dawn to pray,
"O, Lord, heal my husband to your honor and glory.
Thank you ,Lord, for my children and grandchildren.
Lord, help them all to be obedient to the Holy Spirit."
"I have no greater joy than to hear that you walk in the truth."

She goes about her work praising the Lord.
She prepares a tasty breakfast for her ill husband.
She is energetic, a hard worker.
She watches for any needs in the community.
She works far into the night.
She sews for the poor and gives generously to the needy.
She loves to help the elderly at Sunnyside.

She has no fear for her family, because:
"Thou shalt keep him in perfect peace whose
mind is stayed on thee, because he trusteth in thee."
She loves to cut and stitch fine quilts for Shekinah Christian School.
Her own clothes are beautifully made,
especially a blue and white polka dot dress, her husband's favorite.
She is a woman of strength and dignity, and has no fear of old age.

When she speaks, her words are wise,
and kindness is the rule of everything she says.
She encourages her ill husband.
Her children stand up and praise her.
So does her husband praise her with these words:
"There are many fine women in this world,
but you are the best of them all.

Charm can be deceptive and beauty doesn't last,
but your dedication and reverence to God shall be greatly praised.
Praise the Lord for your good deeds and kindness;
because of this, you are praised by your children and grandchildren."
Who is this virtuous woman?
Praise God. She's your mother and grandmother!

Even though we had a policy to discuss it over before any major items were purchased, one time I cheated and went to Darby Buick and traded our car in for a new Buick for Mom's Christmas present. I did not make the switch then. I paid for the Buick and we flew to Plain City for Christmas. Ed Slabach and Willis Miller made the switch, while we were in Ohio. They put the Buick in our carport and put a red ribbon on it, with a card. We got back home to Florida, walked past the car, and she never noticed it. We went in and sat down. Then I said, "Mom, you missed something. Go out and look." She did not look happy or surprised. I said, "Mom, it's your Christmas gift."

She said, "Oh, yes, you knew I would not agree to the trade and you wanted the car. Is it in my name?"

I said "No, I guess not." But I knew in my heart that she appreciated it and still loved me. Oh well, that's the way married life is; you gain some and some you don't. But we were still happily married.

In 1977, our daughter Martha was in Taiwan with Overseas Missionary Fellowship, and we were in the process of getting ready to visit her. We read a lot of books and maps, and checked air flights. After much prayer and planning, we purchased tickets for a 'Trip Around the World'.

The next year, in 1978, Mom and I, along with Carolyn and my niece Ida Plank, went. Mom and I flew to Los Angeles and met Carolyn and Ida, who came there from Columbus, Ohio. We flew from L.A. to Japan, and spent a day in Tokyo. We did a lot of sight-seeing, then boarded a plane for Taipei, Taiwan.

We stayed at a place next to a busy street. Traffic was something else. I went out to count the traffic. Four lanes one way, and a lane for bikes and cycles. I counted between light changes. I don't remember each one, but the total as I remember was over 1300 each light change. In all the traffic, we never saw any accidents. I also walked over to a field where they were planting rice using buffalo.

We flew from Taiwan to Hong Kong and stayed there a few days, then took a bus to the China border. We did a lot of shopping, and toured the city. We flew from there to Bangkok, Thailand. When our taxi driver was taking us to the hotel, he was not very happy. He wanted to go to a different one than we did. I think he would get a cut at his choices. He drove like a maniac. Four lanes of traffic one way. He headed at another car, and Carolyn yelled. He scraped the other car, then he blamed it on Carolyn because she had yelled. But he went right on and never stopped.

When we got to the hotel, he showed Carolyn the damage and said it was her fault. Mom thought right away about me being a bleeder. But the Lord was with us. We stayed at a nice hotel. We were in Bangkok a few days, saw lots of interesting sights and had a ride in a rickshaw. We went to a place where the elephants loaded and unloaded logs with their trunks. One elephant stepped over a man lying on the ground.

Then we flew to India, got there at 2 a.m., and guards with guns were at the unloading ramp. I said to Mom, "What do we want here?" It looked scary. We were sitting in a park one day, when two guys came along. They had long sticks with cotton, and they wanted to clean our ears. They also wanted to shine my shoes. I said it wasn't necessary, and he pointed to my shoes. He had squirted some white stuff on them so he'd have to clean them.

One day we took a trip to the Taj Mahal, all marble and very beautiful. The driver blew his horn at every living thing, even birds. There were all kinds of carts and buggies with horses, mules, donkeys, water buffalo, and oxen pulling them. Women were in the fields of grain, cutting the grain with sycthes, wearing saris. We stopped at a well where they let down buckets for water. One young girl filled a bucket of water, and poured it over her brother to give him a bath. There were monkeys in the trees.

We left New Delhi, and flew across to Tel Aviv, Israel. We had been told a few times that without reservations we would have trouble. But we never did. When we got to Israel, we had to do a little searching for a place to stay, as it was Holy Week. Talk about security; it was tight. Even at the post office you had to be searched before mailing a letter.

We visited the Wailing Wall, and took bus tours of many places of interest. On Sunday we went to church at the Garden Tomb. It was one of the highlights of our trip. We saw a procession of people coming from Bethany to Jerusalem on Palm Sunday.

Before leaving Israel to fly to Frankfurt, Germany, we were searched thoroughly. We landed in Frankfurt and rented a car, and took off for Hanover on the Autobahn. Signs along the highway said "Das is genug", meaning that is fast enough at a certain speed. Mom and I had been to Hanover before, so we thought we knew where we were going. We got on the Autobahn that goes from West Germany through East Germany to West Berlin. We saw a sign that said "U.S. SERVICEMEN NOT BEYOND THIS POINT." We got to a checkpoint, where the gates came down when we entered. The guard came out and checked our passports and said to us "Strocks," meaning "Straight ahead, not left, not right." The gate opened, and we drove on.

As we had been staying in homes for bed and breakfast, we wanted to look for one, not knowing that we were not allowed to get off the highway, as it was only for straight through to West Berlin. We went about ten miles and saw a sign to the town of Gotha, off the road about a mile. We drove into town. It looked spooky. We saw a hotel. No other cars were around, as this was communist East Germany. But we went to the hotel. The owner could not speak English. I told him we wanted two rooms and he said no, one person to a room. He wanted to see our visa, but we did not have one, just a passport. When I wanted to pay with West German money, he said "No, police." I tried to pay with U.S. money, and he kept saying "Police."

He finally assigned us to four rooms. I woke up at 2 a.m., and something told me that we were not supposed to be there. But we could not read the papers we were given, because they were in German. I finally got up at about 6:00 and woke the others and told them, "Let's get out of here; we are not supposed to be here."

We got dressed, and took our luggage to the car. There were no other cars around. It was very spooky outside. But we had not paid our bill. We tried to settle with him, but it was illegal for him to have West German money, and it was illegal for us to have East German money. Finally, seeing we could not settle, he took my money and stuck it way back in the drawer.

We took off for the highway, but we were low in gas. We went about five miles and saw a station that said "Inter-Gas", run by the government for those traveling through. We got gas, and when we went a few miles we wanted something for breakfast. A sign pointed down the road to an inter-

restaurant. We stopped and backed up to go down to this restaurant, but two police saw us and came over and said trouble. We just wanted to go get something to eat. He said, "Follow us." They were very nice and told us how to get back to go to West Berlin. The people inside the restaurant had Russian caps and coats on. We had breakfast, and could pay with our money. We went on our way.

When we arrived at the border of East and West Berlin, we gave them our passports and papers. He asked where we had been, as they allowed five or six hours to pass through on this highway, and we had been gone overnight. We said we had been in Gotha overnight. He went in to get an English-speaking guard and he told us to pull to the side. He said we had not been allowed to get off that highway. We said we did not know. He took our papers and hotel receipts and went back inside. We saw him on the phone. We waited and prayed for one and a half hours, not knowing what the outcome would be. He very emphatically told us again that we were not supposed to have been off that road. I had the receipt from the hotel in Gotha, and showed it to him. I guess he saw we were innocent, and let us go to the next gate. Again, we went through the same thing, but only for about half an hour. He let us go.

Thank you, Lord, we were in free country, West Berlin. We went to the Mennonite unit, Friedensheim and they rejoiced with us that we had been allowed to leave. We had a praise meeting. They told us we were fortunate that we had not been jailed.

We went to Harlem, Holland, and thought we would like a change and go to a hotel that night. We stopped at a hotel. I went in and the prices were too high. Carolyn was driving, and we sat in the car, debating what to do. A man on a bicycle came along and tapped on the window. He said, "Brauchen sie ein zimmer?", meaning, do you want a place to stay? He said to follow him. We followed him on the bike, down through town to a beautiful home. We stayed there, and the price was very low. We had supper and breakfast. She served the breakfast on fine china and silver, very elegant. It was the nicest place we stayed.

We went back to Amsterdam, turned the car in, and flew to London, England. We rode the double-decker bus, and toured the city. We flew back to the U.S., and landed in New York. Praise the Lord for a free country, freedom of worship, and freedom of speech. Freedom of having our family together, as in East Germany many families were separated because of the wall.

We had been gone two months. That summer we made a small apartment on the end of our house on Lafayette-Plain City Rd. We put a kitchen in it, closed the hallway, and put a door in to the outside. We put in built-in cabinets. We then had an auction to sell our surplus furniture and miscellaneous items. We moved into the small apartment. Bonnie and Ivan moved into the big house.

I was on the Mission Board of Son Light Mission and made many trips to Haiti. We went to Haiti in December, and took in the wedding of Miriam and Eris Labady. That was an event you could talk about for the rest of your life. It was a real Haitian wedding. They had a table nicely set with sandwiches, cake, and pop. At first the people went up and got food, but then they crowded in 3-4 deep, and pushed to get food. When they were all done, the table was a mess and the food was all gone. Some people put sandwiches in their purses and came back for more. I'm sure there were some there who hadn't been invited.

After we got back to Plain City, we accepted an assignment with Rosedale Mennonite Missions and Mennonite Disaster Service, and went to Brandenburg, Kentucky as houseparents. We had two girls and five boys. Mom made breakfast, but dinner and supper were furnished at a restaurant.

A tornado had gone through there, and it was very bad. We built two homes, and the local people were very grateful and really appreciated us. Mom and I worshipped at a local Baptist church. We made many friends. Bob Wilsons became very close friends of ours. They even visited us in Plain City later, and we stopped at their house a few times later on the way to Florida. We did a lot of visiting and public relations work. Even if we had many disappointments, we never wished we had not gone there. We still today praise the Lord for those experiences.

While we were in Kentucky, we got a letter from a man in Indiana who wanted to sell us a house in Florida. I called him and he said he wanted to use the money in Haiti. He said the house had three units, all very well equipped and in good shape. So we bought it sight unseen. We sent him a deposit and told him we would come through there and settle for it when we were finished in Kentucky.

We went to Florida and when we went to the house that we had bought, sight unseen, we unlocked the door, embraced each other, and cried. It was a sight. We called Jakie King and gave every piece of furniture to him. It was nothing but junk.

That winter we had our work cut out for us. We made two apartments from the three existing ones. We put in two new baths, a new kitchen, a new roof, new windows, new carpets, and a new heater. We put in insulation, painted the inside of the house, and stuccoed the outside. There was an oil drum in the attic for fuel oil, a real fire trap. After it was all done, we went to Haiti to relax. In fact, we spent more to remodel the house than we had paid for it. So the old saying, "You never get too old to learn," still holds true.

In the spring of 1979, we accepted an assignment to work at World Missionary Press in New Paris, Indiana. They furnished a trailer for us to live in. We really enjoyed that job, packing, labeling, and printing tracts to be sent all over the world.

Our daughter Martha, and Terry Major, were married in October of that year, and Betty and Steve Kaetterhenry the following summer. We finished our house in Florida and bought the house at 2425 Floyd St. from Amos Horst. Ed Slabach and I went to garage sales every Friday and Saturday. At that time the garage sales were genuine, not retail garage sales like they are now. We had a garage sale at our house, and Mom ran it. Ed and I would go garage-saleing, come home with a load of bargains, bring the things in the back door, and add them to the sale Mom was having in the front.

We made another trip to Haiti. I always brought back some Haitian baskets. You could buy them for a few dollars, and we sold them in Ohio for anywhere from $50 to $100 each. I was able to pay for my trip with basket money. Language was a problem in Haiti, but I could hire a little Haitian boy to be my helper. One time I told the boy I wanted a honk-honk horn, like the Model Ts used to have. He took my hand and led me down to the market to a crate of roosters.

One of my favorite stories of Haiti is when we were out in the bush, drilling wells. We had taken our dinner along. Many Haitians gathered around to watch. Willis Miller told me to give some food to a little boy who was very thin and had no shirt. He looked hungry, and I gave him a bowl of cereal. He passed it around to maybe about 25 or 30 others before he took his first bite. I had to cry. Mom had sent some clothes along on that trip. I took one of her dresses, which was a cape dress, and gave it to one of the ladies. She put it on right there, grabbed me and kissed me. She waved her hands, and put on a real show. I hope I will never forget some of these experiences.

I took my brother Ben along one time. We went out to one of the wells that we had drilled. We pumped water, with many Haitians waiting in line with cups to get a cup of water. Ben looked down and cried. As I am writing this, tears come. I have said that every one of our people should go to Haiti to really appreciate what we have here in America.

In the spring of 1981, we bought the house at 376 Bigelow Avenue in Plain City, but we could not get possession of it until late summer. Mom and I planned a trip around the U.S. by way of 'Mennonite Your Way.' We had written to people who had their names in the 'Mennonite Your Way' book. We traveled out west, staying in Mennonite homes in North and South Dakota, Montana, and Oregon. We spent a week at Martha and Terry's in Fernwood, Idaho.

After seeing the Grand Canyon and driving through New Mexico, Colorado, and Kansas, we drove back to Plain City, 'Home Sweet Home.' And even more sweet, because our children had moved us out of the apartment into our new home on 376 Bigelow Ave. Thank you, Lord, that while we were having a great time traveling and enjoying ourselves, the children worked hard to get everything moved and all cleaned for us. That was great.

In the spring of 1982, we remodeled the house on Bigelow Ave. We put in a new kitchen, a new bath, a new roof, new siding, and we added the family room. We spent the rest of the summer working on the house.

Mom and I and Ed Slabachs planned a trip to the New England states for the following summer, 1983. Both being antique-minded, we stopped at lots of antique shops. We went to Pennsylvnia and then to New York, through Maine.

Once we were sitting in a restaurant for breakfast in Portland, Maine, and we went to the cash register to pay. As Ed was anti-credit card, he said he'd give me a dollar if I paid my bill with a credit card. No problem, so I gave them my card, and Ed gave me a dollar. We were laughing about the deal, but I left my card on the machine in the restaurant. We took off and drove about 300 miles to Nova Scotia. We stopped at a motel, and Ed said I should pay with my credit card, as that gets the best exchange rate. I said okay, but I had no card! It was back in Portland in that restaurant. Boy, did Ed laugh. He said, "I don't want to laugh, but I can't help it." After spending about five dollars to trace my card, we used Mom's card. The next morning we traveled through the wooded area of Nova Scotia. Ed was not a believer in spare tires, and we got a flat. Now it was my turn to laugh, and I did. He had to get a pick-up truck with an air-compressor to fix the tire. The bottom line is, we are still good friends.

We spent that fall getting ready to go to Florida. By that time, Plain City was home when we were in Plain City, and Florida was home when we were in Florida. You may have a problem knowing where we lived. I guess one of our daughters put it like it is. In writing her name in her schoolbook, there was a blank for the parents' name and address. She wrote in our names, and said "All over the world."

In 1986 we planned a trip to Papua New Guinea with Nelson and Susie Miller. The reason for going was to visit our daughter Betty, husband Steve, and two children, Rachel and Jeremy. They were working with Wycliffe Bible Translators. Steve worked in the printshop at Ukarumpa, the Wycliffe center.

On October 26 we were taken to the Tampa airport to fly to California on our way to PNG. As we were ready to board the plane at Tampa, our name was paged. We were told that my brother Ben had passed away. We did not have any other choice but to go on, as they were waiting in Port Moresby to take us by plane to Ukarumpa.

We flew to Hawaii, then to Cairns, Australia, and from there to Port Moresby. Steve met us there and they flew us to Ukarumpa. We stayed with Steve's, and Nelson and Susie stayed at the Guest House. Steves took us around the country. We went to a chicken-processing plant, where they had a real assembly line. The chickens were ready for the freezer in about 20 minutes from the time they were killed. Our granddaughter Rachel hugged me and said, "I'm glad I'm not a chicken!" We also went to a mumu, where they cooked a big mound of food by putting it in the ground, along with heated stones, covered it up and let it cook for several hours.

After about a week at Steve's, they drove us over the mountains to the town of Lae. There we stayed at a Wycliffe guest house. We went to see a coffee plantation and processing plant, which was very interesting.

We took our leave of Steve's, and flew to Port Moresby, to Sydney and then flew to New Zealand and landed in Auckland. While there, we went to a Wendy's restaurant. I told the lady that we lived nine miles from the Wendy's headquarters, and she said "You must be from Ohio." She pointed out the owner, and he came to our table. His name was Doug Parker, and he asked us if we knew where the Dutch Kitchen was in Plain City. He said that he married a Mennonite girl from West Liberty, Ohio, and her name was Carol Detweiler. He visited with us at the table, and told the waiter to bring the food. He invited us to his home the next day, that they could show us New Zealand, but we had other plans.

We went to the Agri Dame, where we took in a sheep-shearing show. They had hundreds of sheep, and the guys took turns shearing. I can't recall the minutes it took to shear a sheep, but it was fast. I thought, boy, would Eli N. Troyer of Plain City enjoy that! We also went to a large dairy farm. I think they told us the average dairy farm had around 300 cows. All the cows' tails were cut off. There were no flies, so they didn't need tails. There were large tandem milk trucks.

New Zealand is a beautiful country. The farms are all fenced with trees. I said that if I wanted to be a farmer, I would move to New Zealand. I also said that the Amish make a mistake by not locating in New Zealand. I have been told that they did investigate it, but could not get 'Conscientious Objector' status.

It had been a very interesting trip, and we and Nelsons had a great time. But we had some regrets that we could not be home for my brother Ben's funeral.

In December of that year, 1986, we celebrated our 50th anniversary at the Palm Grove Church. Then we went to Plain City to celebrate our 50th at the Senior Center there. Praise the Lord for 50 years of being together.

In October of 1990, we had a very trying time on our way to Florida. We went by way of North Carolina to stop at Steve and Betty's. While there I was on a ladder cleaning out the gutter, and the ladder slipped and I fell, hitting my head on concrete. I was laid up for a few days, as I am a bleeder. Steve did not want us to go home by ourselves, so he went along to drive.

We were on the road for about two hours, and the car got hot. We had to be pulled into Columbia, South Carolina. They said it was only the thermostat, so we put a new one in, but it got hot again. We went to another garage, and they said we had water in the oil and it needed a new block. It would take a few days, so we rented a car and went back to Steve's.

When they called and said the car was ready, we went again and took the car back. They charged us $950 to fix our car. We took off again, and only went about 200 miles before the car got hot again. We took it to a garage and they charged $90 to take it out and test it. We went about another 100 miles, and the same thing happened again. A trucker from Columbus, Ohio came by and stopped. He went to the next town and sent a wrecker back to take us in. When we got to the town, I asked them how much it would be to haul us to Sarasota. They said $650. I said, "Let's go."

His wife took Steve to the bus station to go back home to North Carolina. We sat with the driver in the truck and headed south. We pulled into our carport at 2:30 a.m.the next morning. I was glad our neighbors were sleeping. The next morning I called Elmer Nolt. "Here is the car. I don't want to see it until it is okay."

One day later he brought it over. I owed him $40, but gave him a $50 bill and told him to keep the change. We used the car and it seemed okay, but we didn't quite trust it. Alvin Mast, Mom's nephew, was there and he went with us out to Coast Cadillac to trade the car in for an '88 Mercury. We had that Mercury until the day Mom quit driving, 7 years later. That trip to Florida was expensive, $2000. I guess that was one of the valleys the Lord let us go through to see our dependence on Him.

In our many travels through the years, home was still the best place to be. 'Home Sweet Home'.

7

In Sickness
and in Health

Later Years

That winter, in 1990, also was the start of declining health for me. First, I had shingles, which I am still suffering from today.

Because of the pain, I took so many pain pills that internal bleeding started. I was taken to Riverside Hospital on Memorial Day weekend. I went in at 4 p.m., and I was bleeding profusely. Doctors were not available, and those there did not know about hemophilia. Mom and I kept telling them that they needed to give me Factor 9, but they kept saying that they needed to find out where the bleeding was coming from. We kept saying forget where it comes from; I just needed Factor 9.

About 10 p.m., they finally were convinced to give me Factor 9. At 11:00 they called Mom to come down and bring her preacher along, as they may have to operate. Mom said that when she and Allen Yutzy, one of our ministers at United Bethel, came down, I was cold and clammy. But then the Factor 9 took hold and the bleeding stopped. I had to have two blood transfusions. At one time, the doctor told the nurse to listen to Mom, because she knows what she's talking about. Even the lady who holds the meetings about hemophilia admitted that we as severe bleeders know more about it than some doctors. I had many times of bleeding in my life. After Factor 9 was developed, it was a real asset.

Also in the 1990s I was starting to have eye problems. First, I had cataract surgery, and then later, a cornea transplant. The cornea transplant was not successful, so I had several laser surgeries, but to no avail. I also had glaucoma. I still have glaucoma and have been using drops for about 18 years now. In about the mid-nineties I was declared legally blind. I could not drive anymore, and a little later I couldn't read anymore. But my 'seeing eye sweetheart' drove for me and willingly read to me. This situation was hard to accept, and I have had many discouragements. But because I knew the Lord had me at heart, and with my sweet wife and my children, grandchildren, and the church helping me, I could still enjoy life.

A difficult experience I had was in Sarasota where I went to the hospital for eye surgery. It was supposed to be done at 7:00 a.m. I was on the table, when the doctor came in and said, "Are you ready for this?" I guess they knew I am a bleeder.

He went to the lab to check, and came back and said that he would not do the surgery. It only tested 15, even though they had given me one dose of Factor 9. So they gave me another dose of Factor 9. They had to wait another hour to check again. They checked it, and the doctor said no, as it only tested 22. They would have to give me another dose. But they were out of it, and had to send to Tampa for more. It was late afternoon when it arrived, and they gave it to me. They tested again, and said they would do it because it now tested 28. I was lying on the operating table all day. At 5 o'clock, they did the surgery and there were no problems.

Because of these transfusions, I was later taken to the hospital and was told I had hepatitis C, which I had contracted from the transfusions. They drained two quarts of fluid from me, and told me that the only thing for me to do was to take Interferon shots three times a week, as the hepatitis had affected my liver. I had cirrhosis of the liver.

We went to the doctor's office two or three times a week for three years for the shots. He had warned me I would get sick after each shot, and that I would threaten to quit. He was so right. I thought I might as well die from not taking the shots, as taking them. But I struggled on. After two years, they tested me and it was good. So I quit for one year, was tested again, and had to start the shots again. I took them for another year and a half, but only half-strength. Then I tested again, and it was clean. So I have not taken them since.

Sometime during this time, I had a large tumor in my scrotum. The doctor said we needed to take care of that, even though I was a bleeder. He sent me to a specialist, who said we had to do surgery. That was a Friday. I told him we would go home and discuss it with the family. He said he expected to hear from us on Monday. On the way home, the idea of annointing came to my mind. Mom asked if I had thought about annointing, and I said that yes, I was just thinking about it.

We went home and called Walter Beachy, our pastor. He said we could plan for it the following morning. As they had me come up and sit on a chair, Walter explained it to the church and asked me if I had anything to say. I said that if the Lord heals me, praise the Lord. But if not, He will have something better for me.

It was a sight to see all the people coming up and laying hands on me; I can hardly write this because of tears. I was annointed on Sunday. Monday morning I called the doctor and told him that they had annointed me, and I was going to let the Lord take care of it. He said I had his blessing. In ten days the tumor was totally gone, and there's been no trace of it since.

At church a few weeks later, the church choir came up front and sang the Hallelujah Chorus, and that was a real blessing. As I walked out, someone said that was for real. "Don't you wonder why the Lord does not heal your eyes?" I don't know, but He must have a reason, as He makes no mistakes. But I do know that if I stay faithful to the end, someday He will give me perfect sight. Praise the Lord.

Some time later, one morning in our devotions, the Lord laid a vision on my heart. That was to start writing to persons to encourage them. I thought, oh, I can't write. He reminded me that He would help me. To whom, He would reveal to me by the Holy Spirit. My daughter Carolyn said, "Dad, don't just write to friends, but listen to the Holy Spirit to tell you to whom."

She made me stationery with big black lines and my name in large print, and gave me a dozen 20/20 pens. Having been so discouraged at times, I figured it was worth a try. So I started writing, and now I have written to many people, young boys and girls, pastors, and many times to young boys who are hemophiliacs. It has been such a blessing. When Mom reads the paper and The Budget to me, I catch names of people with problems. I feel now that if the Lord would have healed my eyes, I would not be doing this. Thank you Lord.

After returning from Florida in the spring of 2000, we decided to take care of a hernia I had had for about two years. On June 16, we went to the hospital. I had to have 5 injections of Factor 9 before the surgery.

On August 12, 2000, in the morning, Mom and I were riding our bikes to the Dutchman Restaurant, then to Super Duper grocery store. Just before we got to the store, Mom hit a pothole and fell over on her bike. She was first taken to Marysville Hospital and they took her to Doctor's West Hospital. She suffered a lot. Her shoulder was torn out of the socket and she had a broken right arm. They were able to put the socket back in place without surgery, which we praise the Lord for. Her arm was put in a sling. We were a helpless couple. The church people brought in meals. Karla, our granddaughter, wanted to take care of Grandma, and she came in every day for a time, and other friends came in to fix her hair. The children and friends became very special to us. I shed tears many times because of what people did for us.

We were getting back to about normal, when on September 20, we went to Super Duper and I started getting pain. We called Carolyn and she took us to the doctor. He rushed me to the hospital. I had a strangled hernia on my other side. The doctor worked on it and got it back in place. They said we could take a chance that it would not happen again. I did not want to take the chance for pain like that again, so we decided to do surgery. They gave me three injections of Factor 9, and then the nurse came to the house for three more injections. After such a summer, we were ready to go back to Florida.

The year 2001 was the year of our big trip to Iowa and Wisconsin. After much prayer and encouragement by the children, we decided to accept Jake and Lydiann's offer to take us, in their motor home, to Iowa, where we had lived for four years in the early years of our marriage.

We left in August. The motor home was equipped with two single beds in back, a shower and toilet. It was air-conditioned. Jakes had a bed in front, also two lounge chairs and a breakfast table. It was really a good deal. Martha and I could lie on the beds as we traveled. The first day we drove to Lester Detweiler's at Evansville, Wisconsin. We got there about five p.m. They had invited a number of our relatives and friends to the house. We had homemade ice cream and all kinds of desserts. We had a very good evening. We parked the motor home at their place for the night. It was hot, but we had air-conditioning.

After breakfast in the motor home we drove to Cashton. We visited with Levi and Wilma Miller. Wilma is my niece. We then went to Wilton where we visited with David Yutzy, my nephew. We also visited Levi and Elizabeth Shetler. Elizabeth is my niece. We went to a campground and parked there for the night.

The next morning, Jake made eggs and bacon for breakfast. We went on to Livingston, where we went to Daniel and Martha Yoder's. Daniel is Jr. Yoder's son and Martha is my sister-in-law Ada's daughter. They have two cute ponies that their children had a lot of fun with. Daniel and the boys were in Lancaster a few miles away doing roofing. After a nice visit with Martha and the children, we stopped in town to talk to Daniel. This was a very interesting stop.

We then left for Buchanan County, Iowa. We got to Clarence and Ada Miller's place about 5 p.m. Ada's Freeman, Eli, and some others came there and we had a meal and a very good visit. Clarence was lying down and did not feel well. I had a picture of my brother Jonas that I had taken when he still lived, and his children and grandchildren really enjoyed that picture, as most had never seen him. He had been a hemophiliac, and died when his children were very young. It was a very good evening. It brought back many good memories.

The next morning we went to the farm where we had lived for four years, from 1946 to 1950. Adin Helmuth, my nephew, lives there now, and they gave us a good tour of the farm. The house has been changed a lot. We have many good memories from the time we lived on this farm. We stopped at the school where Jake, Bill, Carolyn and Betty went to school and had a good visit with the teacher.

We went to all my nieces' and nephews' in Buchanan County. Eli Helmuth, my nephew, is a preacher and in poor health. We also went to Amanda's, the widow of Wayne Yoder. Wayne had been a schoolmate of Jake and Bill. Then on to a new restaurant that was built on the Dan Bontrager farm.

Jake made a good breakfast again the next morning. This was now Saturday. We drove around, visiting friends and relatives. We went to some of the Amish stores where they sell crafts and furniture, made by the Amish. At some of the places they came out to the motor home. At one place the whole family of ten came in the motor home. We had the air-conditioner on, and they liked that.

We got up early the next morning as we wanted to go to the Amish church. It started at 9 a.m. Church was held at Allen Detweiler's. Allen is my nephew. When we got there, they did not have to unhitch our horse, but they gave us a special place to park our rig. We got a lot of attention, but they treated us royally. We had some questions about sitting on those hard benches for three hours, but they gave us rocking chairs to sit on. Jake wanted to sit with the men in the main room, but Martha, Lydiann and I sat on the porch. They had a normal Amish service, very low and slow. We understood most of what was said and sung. After it was over, they motioned us to go out, and they wanted to have a 'shtill hokka'. That means a members' meeting to discuss personal things. For dinner they put us out on the porch with the boys, but the peanut butter, pickles, and 'roht-reeva' (pickled beets) were good.

After they dismissed, they came to us and greeted us and really seemed to be glad to see us. Out in the yard under the shade tree we had a great time telling stories, reminiscing of the years we had lived there. Fannie Lehman told about when she had worked for us when one of our children was born. I think we paid her $3 a week. After many stories and lots of fond memories, we left to go to Kalona, about 100 miles south, and spent the evening with Ed and Nona Slabach.

The next day we left Kalona and drove to Canton, Missouri, where John and KatieYutzy live. Katie is my sister. John had a stroke a few years ago, and couldn't talk, but we had a good visit. John seemed to be happy, but could only motion. He has since died. We visited three of John's children and their families. One has a harness shop and one has a craft store.

We then drove to the Mississippi River and watched the ships go through the locks and the levee. We ate the evening meal there. Then we drove to Hannibal and parked at a Wal-Mart store for the night. After breakfast the next morning, we drove back to Plain City, and arrived home on Tuesday evening around 7 p.m.

Thank you, Lord, for a beautiful trip, and thanks to Jake and Lydiann for encouraging us to go, and for the way they so beautifully took care of us. We won't soon forget that trip. The Lord was with us all the way. But home is still 'Home Sweet Home'.

Even though I am legally blind, I am so thankful to the Lord for a good memory and the ability to write. I spend most of the year writing and taking care of the apartments, visiting friends and getting visitors. Friends are so kind in picking us up to go to special occasions.

In closing these writings, I want to say in my earlier years, I lived a life of recklessness and lived a life not too good. I lived in sin at times, and I accept the responsibility for my many mistakes. I want to say that I blame no person or church for the way I lived. It was my choice at the time. But I want to thank the Lord for having mercy on me, and for giving me the grace to repent and make restoration. Praise the Lord.

8

Stories and Poems

A Pretty Girl

A pretty girl, Martha, lived on Amish Pike.
Thinking, that girl I think I would like.
I sent someone to ask her for a date.
She said that's OK, I think that would be great.
But that would be a long way to go,
For she is the daughter of One-Armed Joe.
December 10th, 1936, Martha became my wife.
Walking together was a whole new life.
The Lord blessed me with a beautiful treasure,
Living with Martha has been a real pleasure.
1937, Louella, a cute baby girl was born.
She died seven months later; our hearts were torn.
Knowing that she went to heaven to stay,
We have the assurance we can meet her some day.
1938, The Lord blessed us with Jake, a baby boy.
That brought Mom and me a lot of joy.
We were farming and were much in debt.
Mom always encouraged me not to fret.

continued on next page

1939, Willie was born, a cute little lad.
The $25 to deliver him was not to be had.
Now we were a family which totaled four.
Financially, we were very very poor.
1941, The Lord blessed us with Carolyn, very much alive.
That made our family be a total of five.
Financially, we were able to see light;
Although money was still very tight.
We lived on a farm down Amlin Way,
Quite a distance for a horse named Nay.
We all worked hard and put in a long day,
Thinking, somehow, it would pay.
1942, a baby girl, Betty, was born.
Years later she helped us husk corn.
1944, a big-eyed baby girl came to stay.
Dad was not home, had gone to an auction that day.
That year we got a Chevrolet car;
For a horse and buggy it was too far.
We got a tractor and farmed more land.
Our family of seven worked together, hand in hand.
Two year later, we sold out and moved out west,
Thinking for our family, that would be best.
Back to horse and buggy we did go.
That was rough, because of the ice and snow.
We all worked together and worked hard;
We butchered hogs and we even made lard.
We made new friends and enjoyed them much.
We all worked like the Pennsylvania Dutch.
Financially, we were able to see light,
Because money became a little less tight.
Mom was a hard worker and a super cook.
I am so glad in 1934, I took that second look.
Two girls and one boy were stillborn.
We now have four children on Heaven's shore.

That behooves us all to live the Lord's way;
Then we can meet them all some day.
Thinking back on those four years,
We no more had any financial fears.
Moving back to Ohio was our plea,
And the family did very much agree.
We got a car again, and joined U.B.
We think that was a wise choice, as you can see.
1950, a darling little girl, Martha, came to stay,
But she was rushed to the hospital the same day.
She was very, very sick;
They changed her blood real quick.
1952, Bonnie was born, as cute as a doll,
But she could very easily bawl.
Bonnie became Jake's little pet.
With his truck ran in the ditch, remember that yet?
Thank you, Lord, for blessing us 65 years,
For your love and grace can't be bought at Sears.
Thank you, Mom, for being submissive for 65 years,
For your love and prayers, and for your tears.
Thank you, children, for your faith in the Lord.
Special is the family that is of one accord.
Oh, yes, I dare not to forget
About Carolyn, has Sara for a pet.
Thank you, Lord, for all the traveling we could do,
All made possible, because of blessings from You.
Now that our health is failing, and living alone,
We have the assurance God is still on the Throne.
To the children, grandchildren,
and great-grandchildren, too,
We dearly love every one of you.
Oh yes, Clara, will you forgive me,
Because you are also part of our family.
John said, "Having believing children gives great joy."
Martha, for 65 years, you have given me great joy.

The Sugarcreek Budget

The Sugarcreek Budget is very important to us,
To get the Budget in Florida is quite a fuss.
But a kindly old gentleman came up with a plan,
This kindly old gentleman goes by the name Dan.
He gets The Budget right off the bus,
And delivers The Budget to our house for us.
This Good Samaritan lives at 3439 Gardenia Street;
His hospitality and kindness is hard to beat.
His wife is a very capable Budget scribe;
She is an offspring of the Cornelius Beachy tribe.
Dan delivers The Budget with his three-wheel bike,
That kind of service we really do like.
Dan and Katie Hostetler are an interesting pair,
Many interesting stories they like to share.

John and Annie

I want to tell you of a special miracle the Lord performed. I was sitting on the porch, watching people go by, when a fellow drove by on a bicycle. I yelled, "Come in here and tell me who you are." He turned around and came in. We started playing the Mennonite game: Whom do you know? Whom do I know? We talked for about an hour. He told me he came from Goshen, Indiana. His wife's name was Maggie.

One day they had gone out to eat, and after returning home, Maggie went upstairs and he stayed downstairs. He wanted to ask her a question, so he called, "Maggie." No answer. He went to the stairs and called her again. No answer. He went upstairs, and his wife had died.

The man got off his bike and hugged me and said, "Thank you for stopping me. I am a lonely man." Then he left.

His name was John Graber. He lived in an apartment down the street. Two days later I woke up at 2 a.m. and the Lord seemed to tell me that maybe John would make a good husband for Annie Mast. Later, Mom and Annie went out shopping, and on their return, we were sitting around the table, visiting. "Annie, could I introduce you to a man here in Sarasota?"

"No," Annie replied. After a few minutes, she said, "As a friend only." I thought, well, friendship always comes first.

A few days later I biked up to John's apartment. I said, "John, could I introduce you to a fine lady here in Sarasota?"

He replied, "Only as a friend. Where does she work?"

"At the Dutch Oven."

"Oh, there's a lady who lives two doors over from me who works there."

"That's her," I replied.

"Oh," he said, "You can't touch her with a ten-foot pole."

"Oh, yes, she can be touched, but she is always on the run, and is a little bit flighty."

"When can we go down to meet her?"

"You're the driver. You say."

"Let's go Monday morning. I'll pick you up."

Monday morning we went to the restaurant to meet her. She came out of the kitchen, and we had a good time introducing them to each other. About a week later, Annie called Mom and said, "Pray for me. John wants to take me out to eat." A few weeks later Annie called again and said, "Pray for me. John wants to take me out to eat again."

John took Annie to Orlando to a party for John's grandson's birthday. Annie said the grandson walked around holding Annie's hand and calling her Grandma. Later we heard that John and Annie were sitting together in church. They called us and wanted to go to the Palm Grove Church, and they sat together. I later told them I had written a poem about them. This is the poem:

The Dutch Oven is a good place to eat,
Also a good place for John and Annie to meet.
As John walked in to get something to eat,
Annie came from the kitchen for John to meet.

John and Annie kept seeing each other.
One thing for sure, they did not have to ask Mother.
As John and Annie prayed and served the Lord,
By now they could see they were of one accord.
To Orlando they went to see John's son,
To see if they should continue with their fun.
John is blessed with a wonderful family;
Annie loves that, as you can surely see.
Annie also has a very nice clan,
All this make John and Annie walk hand in hand.
This all is surely in God's will,
So it will be easy for Annie to say, "I will."
"Thank you, Lord, for bringing John in my life,
Help me to be a super-good wife."

On a Thursday evening they stopped in and wanted to read the poem. "No, it's too early," I said.

"Come on." they said. "We want to read it."

"Okay, if you insist."

The reason I did not want them to read it was because the last two lines read that this must be the Lord's will, so it would make it easy for Annie to say "I will."

They read it, and then John took Annie's hand and told us, "That's just what she said. You are invited to our wedding, June 20th, in Goshen, Indiana."

Jake and Lydiann took us to the wedding. It was very touching. Before they were united, all John's children and Annie's children went up on the stage and sang "Bind Us Together." Annie's son-in-law Lonnie preached the sermon.

They are a super-fine couple. I have no doubt the Lord put them together. They are now married three years, and John told me later that he can't believe that a wife could make him so happy.

I have had many interesting experiences by asking someone who they are, but this was my best one.

Stories of the Times

1945

"Mom, look who just drove in, Amos Bontrager and their four children... Now look again, in here come Joe Yoders and their six children. Jake, go out and help them unhitch. And look, Mom, here come Levi Yoders and their six children. Willie, now it's your turn to go help unhitch. Come on in, you folks, we are so glad to see you."

"Carolyn, run to the cellar and get two more cans of peaches, and Betty, you go out to the smokehouse and get a ring of sausage. Jake, go out to the pump house and get a pail of water. You folks make yourselves at home. We are so glad you came. Amos, I suppose you have all your crops in. How about you, Levi?"

"I have five acres of corn to put in. If it doesn't rain, I'll get that done tomorrow."

"We have ten acres to put in yet."

"Dinner is ready," Mom says. We all gather around the table.

"I see there are 29 of us. If you put little Johnny on the high chair, we'll make it. Thank you, Lord, for the food and all those around this table. Now, everyone help yourselves to the food."

"Mattie, that was a delicious dinner; that pie was so good. You children can go out and play with the pony, but be careful; he is a little spooky at times."

"Well, Eli and Mattie, it is time to go as we have a lot of chores to do. Come and visit us sometime."

"Mom, that was a good day. I really did enjoy that. Boys, it's time to go after the cows and feed the hogs; don't forget to gather the eggs. Put the lantern in the chicken house. Also, be sure to cool the milk good. Oh, yes, you have to start the windmill too."

1950

"Mom, how about inviting some folks to come for dinner after church?"

"That would be okay. But I'll have to go to the store for a few things."

"Hello, Chauncey. Would you like to come over for dinner after church?"

"Yes, we would love to."

"Hello, Sanford, would you love to come for dinner after church?"

"Yes, we would, but don't go to too much trouble."

"We won't. Hello, Abe. Would your folks want to come to our house for dinner on Sunday?"

"We sure would."

"Mom, isn't it nice that we as brothers and sisters in the Lord can come together and visit and fellowship? Now that we are all around the table, we are so glad you came. Chauncey, would you ask the blessing? Everyone help yourselves as long as it lasts. Wasn't that a good sermon we heard today? Oh, yes, next week the Brunk tent meetings start in Wooster. I think we'll go. Thank you all for coming. May the Lord bless you all."

1970

"Mom, let's invite some folks for a snack after church tonight."

"Ok," Mom says.

"Leon, come to our house after church tonight."

"Okay."

"Omar, come to our house tonight after church. Lonnie, would you folks come visit us after church?"

"Shall we bring something?"

"No, we have plenty of food in the freezer and refrigerator."

It is so interesting around the table, to talk about the world problems, the church service, etc. "It has been a great evening, and thanks to all of you for coming."

It's beautiful for families to come together and fellowship and talk about happenings in years gone by.

1990

"Hello, Sam. How about coming over Sunday for a snack and fellowship?"

"We would love to, but the boys are playing on the Little League and we should go watch them play."

"Hello, Dan, we would like for you to come over Sunday evening for supper and fellowship."

"Well, thank you very much, but there is a special program on TV and we would hate to miss it. Maybe some other time."

"Hello, Mose. Mom and I would like for you and your family to come to our house Sunday evening for a meal."

"We would like to take a raincheck, because we are so busy with other things. We are just too tired out."

"Well, Mom, I guess everyone is so busy with more important things to do. So I guess we will just stay at home, and you can read to me. I appreciate so much when you read to me."

I Am a 1918 Model

My headlights are getting very dim;
My top is getting skinny, and very thin;
My fuel tank needs repair;
My shocks needs replacing;
My brakes are getting thin;
The only thing that works good is my horn.
But I have been promised a brand new model that never wears out,
and needs no repair.
My body will last forever.
In the meantime, the Lord has given me a spare,
who reads to me, cooks, and loves me,
and children who keep me rolling.
So I am still pretty well off.

Garage Sales Are Not My Cup of Tea

by Noah Gingerich, printed by permission

Garage sales and yard sales, you'll find them everywhere,
You can't go any place that they are not there.
In cities, in villages, and on the countryside,
In every community nationwide.
To go to these places everyone is free,
But garage sales are not my cup of tea.

Some folks are addicted to go to these places
And at many of them you'll see the same faces.
To go to them I'm sure is no sin
And also to a few of them I have been.
But never have I gone on a garage sale-ing spree,
For garage sales are not my cup of tea.

It's a good way to get rid of your surplus they say
So they'll set a date for a garage sale day.
Tack up a few signs and maybe run an ad
And expect people to be stopping like mad.
But in this group you're not apt to see me
Because garage sales are not my cup of tea.

If ever there is a garage sale at our house
It'll be against the wishes of my wife's spouse.
Should it come to this, I'd say of course
There'll be no separation or divorce.
And though we still should somewhat disagree,
Garage sales still are not my cup of tea.

Garage Sales Are My Cup of Tea

A Response to Noah Gingerich's Poem

Saturday morning to garage sales we go,
Mom and Dad with children in tow.
Toys and games and books galore,
More enjoyable than going to the store.
Dishes for Mom, tools for Dad,
If you bought them new, it would be so sad.
It's amazing what you can see;
That's why garage sales are my cup of tea.

The children need clothes, and shoes we have to buy;
To the store we go, but prices are high.
Let's stop at a garage sale down the street,
Lots of goodies and shoes for the feet.
The savings we experienced were truly great;
We had money left, so we stopped and ate.
We all were happy and had money left, you see;
That's why garage sales are my cup of tea.

continued on next page

Prices on furniture are very high,
No payment till the first of July.
It can also be put on a credit card.
Making payments can get very hard.
Let's try a garage sale where prices are low,
So you pay cash with no payments, you know.
Occasionally, some things are free;
That's why garage sales are my cup of tea.

At Mt. Hope is a big sale planned,
Quilts, lots of nice things at hand.
All proceeds to go for Haiti's poor,
As we buy, we'll receive a blessing, I'm sure.
Lots of friends you're sure to see;
That's why garage sales are my cup of tea.

Some say garage sales are not their cup of tea,
But hauling people is not for me!
Some shuffle, some like to fish,
I love to scrounge for an antique dish.
At garage sales you have a good chance
Of finding some for just a few cents.
I have found a few for a small fee;
That's why garage sales are my cup of tea!

Local Man Remembers Village of Years-Gone-By

(Printed in The Plain City Advocate, as a Guest Columnist)

B eing legally blind, I thank the Lord for a good memory. I like to reminisce and I thought I would take a trip to town and pay tribute to the early businesses and owners that played a large part to make Plain City the biggest little town.

I hitch my horse to the buggy for a trip to town. Passing Forest Grove Cemetery, I am reminded of the time we Amish boys trimmed grass around the tombstones for one cent each. I go on to town, hitching my horse on a hitch rack and putting a blanket on my horse to keep him comfortable. I go to Dan Cheny's Grocery, where Rummell and Brill is now located, to get coffee. "How do you want it ground?" This coffee was for our Sunday morning breakfast - coffee soup.

Next to where the dime store was, now Yoder's Variety. Here I get a pound of chocolate drops for nine cents a pound and four packs of chewing gum for a dime, to take to my girlfriend's house, now my wife of 65 years!

Next door is the Farmer's National Bank, run by Cephas Atkinson, one of the main places in town, now owned by Citizen's National with Mary Mitchell as vice-president.

I go to the end of the 'flatiron,' where Cappy Jackson had a gas station that sold gas for 17 to 20 cents a gallon. Around the corner, in the same building was Johnny Michael, one of my heroes. He sold me the house on South Chillicothe Street where Mrs. Robert Lombard now lives, for $9,000.

Crossing the street I pass John Gaa's ice house. He was also the 'milk hauler.' Next door is Dr. Eli Holmes, who was very well known. He came to our house with his old Model-A to deliver two babies for us at $20 each. He was next to the store under the clock. Howland Hardware, owned by M.D. Norris, sold anything from oil lamps to gas Maytag washers, which were delivered by Roman Miller. Howland's is now owned by Perry Yoder.

Across the alley is the Brigg Mercer Building. Brigg sold farm machinery and clerked at auctions. That building is now Plain City Auction, owned by Dave and Rhoda Helmuth.

Down the street, on Church Street was Dr. Herman Karrer. Doctor and Margaret Karrer were special to us as he took a lot of interest in my hemophilia problem and delivered two babies for us.

Crossing over to North Avenue was the Fee Brothers Milling Company, handling grain and making flour. It is now an apartment building.

I head back to Main Street and pass Ferguson Funeral Home, owned by Jay Ferguson. This is probably one of the oldest businesses in Plain City, and is still owned by the Ferguson family. Next I come to George Elias' store. Next door was Ben Jones' drugstore where we bought five-cent ice cream cones.

I go to North Chillicothe Street, where Bob Jackson had a well-known furniture store. Crossing the street on the corner is Scoby's Restuarant. I eat at the corner restaurant, a good eating place for the local businessman.

Crossing the alley, on the corner were George Spiger and Herbie Clark. They sold all kinds of shoes, overshoes and clothing. That place is now occupied by the gun shop.

On the same block was Joe Hofbauer. Joe and his wife, Anna, butchered their own hogs and cattle and sold them at the store. Joe was from Germany and was a favorite of the community.

Next door was Hamburger Inn, run by Harold Page. You could buy two hamburgers, fries, and a milkshake for a dollar. Right next door was Beckman Poultry, buying and selling eggs and chickens. In the same block, Lucas Drug Store was owned and run by Howard Lucas. They had a complete list of prescription drugs and pharmacy needs.

Next is the Lovejoy Plaza Block, A&P Grocery and the post office. First class letters could be mailed for three cents.

Crossing the alley, I see Tuny Andrews and Graber Garage. You could get a good tune-up for a few dollars.

Following West Main Street I come to the Plain City School. Ero Scott and Mrs. Toops were my teachers. Warren Moore was my marble-playing buddy. I think Warren got most of my marbles. No segregation here in this school! No blowing up the school, as Mr. Gower had a good paddle. If you fell victim to this paddle, no telling our parents, as that would call for the same treatment at home!

Heading on west on Main Street I come to the Canning Factory, canning sweet corn, hauled in by horses and wagons. There are lines formed to Main Street, waiting to unload. This is now occupied by the boat factory.

Back downtown to the Early Hatchery, where you buy baby chicks or hatch eggs brought in, owned by Dewitt Simons. Then on down the street to Tedrick's Hardware Store and John Deere dealer. This was a very popular place, run by Harley Tedrick and two sons, Ed and Bob, and salesman Putter Evans. Putter sold me my first new tractor, Model B cultivator, and plow for $750.00. Next door I got my first haircut away from home for 35 cents by Jesse Sellers.

Before leaving town I get my horse shoed by Bill Fitzgerald.

Oh, yes, we dare not forget Johnny Minshall, the little guy that swept the streets and cleaned up the horse droppings. He was also the policeman; there was no speeding or 'hot-rodding' in town. Johnny demanded order, but people liked him.

Heading for home, I stop at Minshall's Grocery in a house on South Chillicothe for a dozen eggs for nine cents and a loaf of bread for eight cents. We were able to charge our groceries and pay for them when the milk check came in.

Now on home to do the chores - milking our herds of cows by hand. Then it is supper time with corn bread on the menu. After supper, we thank the Lord for the day's blessings. We sit down and get news from *The Plain City Advocate*, and then retire for the night on a mattress filled with cut straw that comes out of the straw shed.

Those were the good ol' days!

Forbidden Fruit

(Printed in the Plain City Advocate, as a Guest Columnist, July 2001)

Beautiful is the family bound together by the Love of God. "Bring up a child in the way he should go, and when he is old, he will not depart from it."

Once there was a family of 12. A father, mother and six boys and four girls lived on Bigelow Avenue in Plain City, Ohio.

One morning Dad told one of his sons to go to a far-away land and get some food. "Now, son, do not trespass on forbidden land."

The son took off, and came to a pot of peanuts, which was free for all. But the son saw better food on the other side, but it was forbidden food. The son thought, "No one is looking. I could steal some of that food."

But the man in the watchtower saw him and arrested him and sentenced him to a boys' camp, away from home.

When the son did not return, Dad sent another son and a daughter to see what the problem was. They too passed the food that was free and sneaked to the forbidden area. They too thought the man in the watchtower was not there. But, sure enough, he was hiding inside the window. The son was trapped. The girl got on her knees and begged for mercy.

The judge again sent the son to a boys' camp, but let the girl go on good behavior. "You go home and tell your family about the danger of trespassing and stealing." The girl went home and told them of the danger in sinning.

Now Dad said, "I will send two boys and one girl." And he told them what to do. "One go to the side of the vineyard, one come in from the rear, and one get the owner's attention by surprise. Our plan has got to work." So they went, but the owner's wife was inside the window watching, and the three were caught in broad daylight.

The judge transported all three to a work camp, where they were put behind bars.

"Mom," Dad said. "We have lost half of our family. Just think, Mom, they are out in the world and we do not know where they are. I have an idea, Mom. Let's send two of the girls. The judge will have mercy on them."

"Ok, if you say so," said Mom.

The girls went and they too passed up the pot of peanuts that were for free because the other food looked so good. But the man in the watchtower was watching and caught them in the act again.

The judge said, "I am sorry, girls, but you have been warned and there were signs plainly saying, "Stay Out!" The judge said he was very sorry, but he must send them to a girls' school.

"Oh, Dad," Mom said. "We must find out where our seven children are."

After much debate and discussion, they sent the other two boys and a girl to try to find them. "Bring back some of the free food and don't steal any of the forbidden fruit, even if it does look better."

So they left, and did get some free food. But again it was getting dark, and the owner of the vineyard was probably sleeping. "We will sneak in and get just a little of the forbidden fruit." But again, the vineyard was closely guarded and they were all three caught in the act, and were sentenced to the woods to do hard labor.

So Mom and Dad were alone. Dad said, "Mom, this is all your fault. You should have stayed home and taken care of the family, instead of going to work."

Mom said, "Dad, it's all your fault, as you were not a good influence on them."

"Ok," Dad said, "I am going out tomorrow and tell that owner what I think of him. I am going to give him a piece of my mind."

So Dad took off the next day and upset the can of free peanuts and stormed to the vineyard to show his authority. He jumped down on the can of forbidden fruit and spilled it out on the ground.

The owner was inside the window and saw Dad jump off and on again. After warning him a number of times, he got bolder. Finally, Dad jumped off, right into the trap. Now he was behind bars. Because he had been the leader, the judge sentenced him to be transported out of the country.

The mother is now alone, mourning the loss of her family of 11. The family life has been ruined, but the birds now have freedom to the once forbidden fruit. Eleven of the family are out in the world and the mother is living alone. How sad.

"Be sure your sins will find you out."

This is a story of a family of 12 squirrels that robbed the bird feeder in our front yard.

Children Are a Blessing From the Lord

Jacob Freeman Helmuth is married to Lydiann Miller. Jake and Lydiann have five children and 19 grandchildren. Jake is a builder. Jake and Lydiann both take a lot of interest in their children and grandchildren. They spend much time helping the children.

Special memory: When Jake was 16, we bought a new Nash car. It looked like a bathtub upside down. "Dad, please don't make me use that car, as the young folks make fun of it."

William Helmuth is married to Fannie Yutzy. Bill and Fannie have four children and six grandchildren. Bill is a building contractor; Fannie works at the Dutch Kitchen, keeping the salad bar in tip-top condition. Bill is very much interested in prison ministry.

Special memory: When we lived on the farm on Watkins-New California Rd., Mom and I went to an auction. Our house caught on fire. Bill told the children to keep the doors closed, so there would not be a draft. He ran to the neighbors', barefoot, to call for help. He told us he ran very fast. I said, "Did you pass any cars?"

Carolyn Helmuth is single, but she does have a special four-footed friend. Her name is Sara. Carolyn has a God-given heart for children. She loves to take nieces and nephews to ball games, and she visits people in hospitals. She loves her Mom and Dad very much. She makes many calls to Florida.

Special memory: When Carolyn was in voluntary service in El Dorado, AR, we received some letters that were very special. They are in a box in the attic. She thanked us for teaching her to work, and for demanding obedience.

Elizabeth Helmuth is married to Steve Kaetterhenry. Betty and Steve have two children. Betty spent most of her years teaching school in Michigan, Delaware, Costa Rica, and Bolivia. In Bolivia she met Steve. Steve is a printer at JAARS for Wycliffe.

Special memory: When Betty nearly lost her life at Jeremy's birth, Mom was out in California with them and I flew out to be with Mom and Betty. I had not planned to go, but we believe strongly that the Lord planned it that way.

Edna Helmuth is married to Moses Gingerich. Moe and Edna have two children and four grandchildren. Moe is a retired insurance agent. Edna is involved in buying and selling linens and buttons, and doing quilt shows. Moe is now involved in Wycliffe as a ham radio operator. Moe and Edna enjoy their children and grandchildren.

Special memory: When Edna was a little girl, she would often rub my feet when I would come home from work. She was my special girl, the baby for 7 years, and very much loved.

Martha Helmuth is married to Terry Major. Terry and Martha have three children. They live in New York and Terry is a pastor. They are both very much involved in church work. Martha does quilting, like her mother. Martha spent four years in Taiwan. Trevor, their son, is a special grandson to grandpa.

Special memory: Martha would play with her dolls and teddy bears, lining them up on chairs and seats and teaching them. Also she was called a 'miracle baby' by the doctor because she had to have her blood changed at birth.

Bonnie Helmuth is married to Ivan Yoder. Ivan has had two kidney transplants. They have one son and one daughter. Ivan has a good job with an air-conditioning company. Bonnie worked at Riverside Hospital and with the Borden Company, but is now at Grant Hospital in Columbus.

Special memory: When Bonnie was about five, we were at Niagara Falls. I walked out on some stones, near the water. When she saw me, she yelled, "Dad, be careful! You have my gum in your pocket!"

Prayer of Thanksgiving

Thank you, Lord, for making salvation available to me, through the birth,
crucifixion, and rising again of the Lord Jesus Christ.
My sins are washed away by His blood.

Thank you, Lord, for a Dad and Mom who brought me into this world
and taught me to honor God. They demanded obedience and taught me to work.
Thank you, Lord, for my father-in-law and my mother-in-law,
who accepted me into their family.

Thank you, Lord, for giving me a dedicated and submissive wife, who gets up every morning
at five to pray for me, the children, grandchildren, great-grandchildren, the church, and others.
And every night before we go to sleep she takes my hand,
and tells me she loves me and appreciates me.

Thank you, Lord, for blessing us with seven children and one foster daughter who love us, care
for us, and take us places, especially now that we cannot drive. John said he has "No greater
joy than to hear that his children are walking in the truth."
Thank you, Lord, for Lester Wengerds, who have been like our children, and have so well
taken care of our properties in Florida, doing yard work and taking us to the store.

Thank you, Lord, for the Amish Church in Plain City and Iowa,
for teaching me to be obedient, and who helped us by lending us money.
Thank you, Lord, for the Canaan Church, where I learned the importance of sharing
and visiting the sick.
Thank you, Lord, for Palm Grove Church, who accepted us into their fellowship.
Thank you, Lord, for United Bethel Church, where we have been members for 51 years,
and where we have had many rich experiences. This is still our main church. The church
has prayed for us and many healings were experienced, both physical and spiritual.
We love the church.

Thank you, Lord, for helping me through the years during my many bleeding problems. Thank you for the special healing of a fast-growing tumor when I was annointed, and for helping me in times of discouragement because of my eyesight, for the many friends who have visited us.

Thank you, Lord, again for Martha, who reads to me willingly, as my eyesight has failed. Thank you, Lord, for the hardships and financial struggles through the Depression and earlier years of my life. They have given me more appreciation for what we have, and they have been stepping stones in my Christian life.

Credits

Typing: Rachel Kaetterhenry

Editing: Betty Kaetterhenry

Photos: Moe Gingerich, Steve Kaetterhenry,
    Bonnie Yoder, Mom and Dad's photo collection

Cover Photo: Moe Gingerich

Photo Lay-out and Camera Work: Steve Kaetterhenry

Proof-reading: Kristin Elkinton, Edna Gingerich, Moe Gingerich

Pennsylvania Dutch Words and Phrases: Hank Hershberger